Share a joke with Khushwant Singh
and a million others.
See page 111 for details.

Khushwant Singh, author and journalist, was born in Punjab in 1915. He was educated at Government College, Lahore, St. Stephen's College, Delhi, Kings College and the Inner Temple in London. He practiced briefly at the Lahore High Court before joining the Ministry of External Affairs. He shot to literary fame with his award winning novel *Train to Pakistan* and the two-volumes *History of the Sikhs*. Subsequently, he edited *The Illustrated Weekly of India* (1969-1979), *New Delhi* (1979-1980) and *The Hindustan Times* (1980-1983) with great distinction. He was a Member of the Parliament from 1980 to 1986. Today as India's best known journalist and widely read and syndicated columnist, he enjoys the unenviable reputation of "holding a mirror to our face...of being frank, but not venomous, fearless but not intimidating." According to *India Today*, "Khushwant Singh remains perhaps the most spontaneous commentator and raconteur and has provided Indian journalism with some of its most relaxed, tounge-in-cheek writing."

KHUSHWANT SINGH'S JOKE BOOK-II

Illustrated by Sudhir Dar

ORIENT PAPERBACKS
A Division of Vision Books Pvt. Ltd.
New Delhi ● Bombay

Rs. 25.00

ISBN 81-222-0057-5

1st Published 1990
Reprinted   1990
Reprinted   1990
Reprinted   1991
Reprinted   1991
Reprinted   1991
Reprinted   1991

Khushwant Singh's Joke Book II

© Mala Dayal, 1990

Cover Design and inside illustrations
by Sudhir Dar for Vision Studio

Published by
Orient Paperbacks
(A Division of Vision Books Pvt. Ltd.)
Madarsa Road, Kashmere Gate, Delhi-110 006

Printed in India at
Gopsons Paper Pvt. Ltd., Noida

Cover Printed at
Ravindra Printing Press, Delhi-110 006

On Wit, Humour and Laughter...

Making up jokes is no laughing matter. It is a serious business requiring knowledge, insight and experience of what will make people laugh, what will go flat and fizzle out like a damp squib. First, we have to find out why people laugh. For some, the sight of a person with a big nose, a harelip or a stutter, a pot belly or a game leg is enough to set them laughing. Others, want more action like somebody slipping over a banana skin to have the same reaction. One does not need to have a sense of humour to laugh at these. On the contrary, it betrays a total lack of it.

There are many things that make different people laugh. But trying to analyse laughter is like dissecting a frog. You may see its entrails and whatever else it has inside, but you kill the frog in the process. You should just accept laughter as a phenomenon that releases tension and makes you feel lighter and happier. People of different ages react differently to different situations. A child will laugh when somebody stumbles down the stairs. A grown-up will feel sorry for the same man because he has been through a similar experience. Even among grown-ups, the stimuli for raising a laugh differ nation to nation. Although Europeans have a corpus of ethnic jokes about Jews, Scotsmen, Irishmen and Poles, they regard them as bad form. On the other hand, many of our jokes are aimed at certain communities. We make fun of *Marwaris* , *banias,* *Bawajis* (Parsis), *Mianbhais* and *Sardarjis*. All of them are largely on ethnic stereotypes which have no factual basis. Europeans indulge in black humour making jokes about death and funerals; we in India consider them in bad taste. However, we share the same interest in making jokes about our mothers-in-law and our wives. The wife's brother, *saala*, as the butt of humour is an Indian speciality.

There is a fund of humour in all of us. The more it is sought to be suppressed the more it manifests itself. You forbid a person to laugh and he will laugh all the louder. Thus jokes about Hitler, Stalin, fascism and communism flourished in Russia and Germany. When General Zia-ul Haq imposed military dictatorship on Pakistan, he became the object of ridicule in his country. It was the same in India during the Emergency regime. Mrs. Gandhi became a target of humour when she suppressed the freedom of speech.

Getting a laugh out of other people is easier than being able to laugh at oneself. Only people with self-confidence can afford to laugh at their foibles. At one time (before 'Operation Blue Star') Sikhs rightly boasted of manufacturing the best of *Sardarji* jokes. Since then they have developed chips on their shoulders and take offence at jokes aimed at them. Nevertheless *Sardarji* jokes continue to flourish. Another community which excels in making jokes about itself and continue to do so are the Parsis. There is a sizeable collection of *Bawaji* jokes but they need to be related in Parsi Gujarati. I do not know of any other Indian community which has the self-confidence to poke fun at itself.

Not many people are aware that India has a long tradition of humour right from the times of Kalidas and other Sanskrit writers. Every generation has produced great humourists like Birbal, Tenali Raman and Gopal Bhat. Our *bhands* kept this tradition alive throughout the ages.

I have my own targets to aim at. Besides the powerful and the self-opinionated, I find name-droppers extremely ludicrous. There is hardly an Indian who does not indulge in self-praise and not-so-subtle name dropping. These diseases specially afflict our politicians who are forever dropping hints about their closeness to the Prime Minister, Chief Ministers and the people in seats of authority. In addition, our politicians are also sanctimonious humbugs proclaiming their sacrifices for the country, and dedication to social service. It is not very difficult to deflate their self-esteem with a carefully aimed pin prick. Self praise I regard as a form of vulgarity which is found commonly among my countrymen. They will invariably preface it by words like "although I am saying it myself, but..."

The common man's humour is of a lower order than the humour of a man of sophistication. The educated aesthete will respond to literary allusions, puns and jokes about poets, authors, composers and painters. They will mean nothing to the *hoi polloi*. Our film-going public enjoy jokes of the broadest type. A simple reference to a wife as the Home Minister will bring peals of laughter in an Indian audience. Any situation, where head-strong woman is humbled, makes them roar. Our people have to be educated to understand and enjoy subtle humour.

The most sophisticated journals on humour are *Punch* and *The New Yorker*. They are not merely comic, but highly sophisticated forms of wit, irony, sarcasm which tickle one's fantasy. At times their cartoons are so subtle that it takes a long time pondering over them to catch what they are meant to convey.

There are not many jokes in print that will make you explode with laughter. The best that the print can hope to produce is a wistful smile. For explosions of laughter you have to have them told orally by practitioner of the art of joke telling. Fortunately they are to be found in every establishment and at every cocktail party. I am often asked to tell my favourite joke. I don't have a top favourite but over a dozen which improve with each telling. Unfortunately most of my favourites are unprintable because they are dirty and sex-based. A recent one that is both clean and witty is about Giani Zail Singh.

When he was elected President, Mrs. Gandhi was little concerned by the fact that he could not speak English. So she decided to engage an English-knowing tutor for him. She called a cabinet meeting. Her ministers told her, "Gianiji is the Head of our State; only another Head of State should be allowed to teach him." She accepted their advice and floated a global tender. Amongst the applicants was President Reagan.

"You send Giani to me and I'll teach him English in six months," he wrote back.

So Gianiji was flown to Washington. After six months Indira Gandhi sent Rajiv to the White House to find out how much English Gianiji had picked up and bring him back. He was received by the President.

He asked, "President Reagan, tell me how much English has Giani Zail Singh learnt?"

Reagan replied in *theth* Panjabi, *"Is mundey nu agrezi kadi nahin aonee"*.

Reagan had learnt Panjabi, Giani had not picked up any English.

Khushwant Singh

*T*WO Sardarjis, both students of IIT, Kanpur, were talking about the American astronauts. One said to the other, "What's the big deal about going to the moon—anybody can go to the moon. We are Sikhs—we'll go direct to the sun."

"But if we get within 13 million miles of the sun, we'll melt."

And the first answered, "So what, we'll go at night."

Contributed by Judson K. Cornelius, Hyderabad

*T*WO Sardarjis, one day, were discussing politics in a bar in Jullundur. Sardar Mohan Singh said, "I think Darbara Singh's face resembles a sheep's behind."

Sardar Sohan Singh drew back his fist and thumped him right on the nose. "Why did you do that for? Are you a Congressman?" asked Sardar Mohan Singh.

"No," Replied Sohan Singh, "I am a shepherd."

Contributed by Judson K. Cornelius, Hyderabad

A YORKSHIRE yokel bought his wife a pair of budgies as a gift, but when asked which was the male and which the female he failed to identify them, so returned to the pet shop and asked the shopkeeper the same question. "Easy" said the shopkeeper, "tonight when they are mating creep in on them, the one on top will be the male. Then put a white collar around its neck."

The yokel did exactly that, but the next morning when the local Vicar called to visit, the little budgie called out to him, "So they caught you at it too?"

ONCE Josh Maliahabadi, Firaq Gorakhpuri and other poets were drinking at a bar. Pandit Hari Chand Akhtar who was a teetotaller picked up the wine-list and began to scan its contents. Josh asked him what he was reading. "It is a list of spirits, wines and beers and their prices," replied Akhtar.

Josh, the ever-ready wit remarked: "*Panditji aisey lagtey hain jaisay kee hijda Kok Shastra par raha hai*—Panditji is like a eunuch reading a manual on sex."

Contributed by Judson K. Cornelius, Hyderabad

A LADY teacher of English literature fell in love. Her love was not reciprocated. She put it down as "Loves Labour Lost." She fell in love again, got engaged but the fellow backed out. She put it down as "Much Ado About Nothing." The third time she was luckier and more amenable to her gentleman friend. She recorded the encounter "As You Like It." This was followed by marriage and honeymoon. This time it was "A Midsummer Night's Dream." Her husband added the postscript "The Taming of The Shrew."

Contributed by Prof. Narinder Singh, New Delhi

A CINEMA usher had a sore tooth which he wanted taken out. When he was seated in the chair, the dentist asked him which tooth he wanted extracted. The usher replied: "Balcony, *bayen say teesra*—balcony, third from the left."

Contributed by J.P. Singh Kaka, New Delhi

*T*HIS anecdote comes from Pakistan during the regime of the philanderer General Yahya Khan, famous for his penchant for film actresses. One evening a lady arrived at the Presidential Palace and demanded admission, "I am the actress Tarana," she told the security guard.

"I don't care what Tarana you are," replied the guard, "you have to have a pass to go in."

The lady was incensed and demanded to speak to the ADC to the President. The guard rang up the ADC and was told to let the lady in. Two hours later when she was leaving, the same guard sprang to attention and saluted her. "What a change in your behaviour!" remarked the lady very sarcastically.

"Yes madam," replied the guard, "when you came you were the actress Tarana; now you are leaving you are the Qaumi Tarana (national anthem), so I must salute you."

Contributed by Jasbir Singh Bindra, Ludhiana

"*I*s that 6545224?"

"No, this is 6545225."

"No matter, please call Mr. Sharma from next door."

Contributed by J.P. Singh. Kaka, New Delhi

13

A PUNJABI father gave the following advice to his son about to be married. "*Puttar*—son—if you want things from your in-laws, be sure to pitch your demand high. If you want a cycle, ask for a scooter; if you want a motor cycle, ask for a Maruti. Always ask for something better than you need."

The bridegroom who wanted no dowry, imbibed the lesson. When his father-in-law to be asked him what he wanted, the lad replied, "*Mainnoon kuree dee maan chaheedee hai*—give me the girl's mother."

Contributed by J.P. Singh Kaka, New Delhi

*C*HURCHILL and Stalin were spending an evening together, matching each other drink for drink of *vodka*. During a lively line of conversation, Churchill said more than he ought about the Russian ideology. So scathing was he about communism that the Marshall brought the meeting to an abrupt close and said a cold good night.

Next morning, Churchill awoke with a terrific headache and with only a vague memory of what had happened. Gradually it dawned upon him that he owed Stalin an apology for the things he had said about the Russian way of life. So he instructed his secretary to call upon the secretary of the Marshal and tender an apology.

This done, Churchill's secretary was about to leave the Kremlin when the Communist official called him back. He said, "You know, actually Mr. Churchill didn't have to worry. You see the only other person who overheard the conversation between him and the Marshal was the interpreter— and he's dead."

Contributed by Judson K. Cornelius, Hyderabad

*T*HREE friends, a Hindu, a Muslim and a Sikh, were discussing intimate matrimonial problems. How best to send a signal to the wife that the husband desired her company?

"I have evolved a formula," said Rehman. "All I have to say it, 'Begum, you are looking like a newly-wed bride'—and she knows what I have on my mind."

"I have a similar formula," said Sham Lal. "I ask her if she is wearing the same sari she wore on the wedding night. She gets the signal."

"Why this *gol mol,* round-about approach?" questioned Banta Singh. "When I want her company, I simply ring the bell and she comes over to my room."

"This is wonderful," agreed his friends. "But how does she communicate to you that she wants your company?"

"She has her own formula," replied Banta Singh. "She asks me, 'Sardarji, *tuseen ghantee tay naheen vajaaee?* Sardarji, did you ring for me?"

Contributed by J.P. Singh Kaka, New Delhi

*O*NCE when approaching Athens the airhostess announced for the sixth time that they were entering the outskirts of the city. Asked an irate passenger, "When do you expect to leave the outskirts and enter the skirts?"

Contributed by Enjeli Mitra, Hyderabad

15

SHERLOCK Holmes' wife being very neglected took to compensatory eating and put on an enormous amount of weight. The master detective took her to his friend Dr. Watson for examination. After the doctor had given her a thorough examination, Holmes asked him, "What is the problem, doctor?"

"Alimentary, my dear Holmes," replied Dr. Watson.

Contributed by Anil Aggarwal

THE ancient Greek poet, Palladus, wrote:
"Marriage brings a man only two happy days.
The day he takes his bride to bed and the day
He lays her in her grave."

ACTOR-wrestler Dara Singh, taking a stroll along Juhu beach, was set upon by a dozen urchins who after beating him black and blue took away his purse which, fortunately for him, contained very little money. Dara who had floored world's best wrestlers put up no resistance. When he arrived home with two black eyes, puffed cheeks and a torn shirt, his Sardarni asked him in great alarm as to what had happened. Dara Singh told her all. "And why didn't you hit back? Surely you could have knocked the hell out of these skinny fellows!"

"Sure!" replied the Sardar, "But my fee for flooring champions is Rs. 25,000. I don't fight free."

Contributed by Wazir Chand Didi, Chandigarh

*T*HE great modern surrealistic painter **Salvador Dali** was asked, "Do you know what modern art is?"

"You decide to buy a painting to hide a section of the wall where the paint has a tendency to peel. And then, after examining a good 50 paintings, you tell yourself that really it would be prettier to leave the wall the way it is," replied the great master.

Contributed by Reeten Ganguli, Tezpur

A YOUNG entrant to the army was posted at a non-family station for many years. When he got news of a son born to his wife left in the village, he entertained his pals and told them that he had decided to name his son **Pandey.** "Why?" asked his friends.

"In our village neighbours are very co-operative," he explained, "and so we number our children according to their vicinity. If it is neighbour number two, we name the child Dua, if it is number three, he is named Trivedi; number four Chaturvedi. In my case, it was neighbour number five, so he is named Pandey."

His friends were non-plussed. "What if it is the produce of a mixture of neighbours?"

"Then we call him *Mishra.*"

"Disgusting!" they remarked. "What if the paternity is unknown?"

"That's very simple, we name him *Gupta.*"

"What happens if the mother is too shy to divulge the identity of the father?"

"Then we name him *Sharma.*"

Contributed by Manohar Bhatia & Kanwal Kaur, New Delhi

18

A RUSSIAN speaking Indian who spent a few days in Moscow recently, tells me that Russians have begun to laugh at their sacred cows like Karl Marx, Lenin and Communism. When the Soviet leader, Boris Yeltsin, visited the United States last month he told an American audience: "Communism is just an idea, a pie-in-the-sky. We shouldn't try to implement it here on earth."

*Q*UESTION: What is that the United States and the Soviet Union have in common?
Answer: The rouble is not worth anything in either country.

*T*WO Hindi speaking friends who were trying hard to learn English decided to correspond with each other in *angrezee*. The first letter went somewhat as follows: "My dear *mitr*, I am in the well. I hope you are also in the well."

Contributed by A.K. Sharma, Patiala

*S*ANTA gave Banta a letter to post. Banta looked at the envelope which was full of details like son of, village, *dakkhana*, tehsil, district and state. "Why do you have put all this on the envelope?" he asked.

"I receive letters with no more details on the envelope than my name and country: Santa Singh, India."

"Wonderful! How is that?"

"*Dustee*—by hand," replied Santa calmly.

Contributed by Harish Monga, Ferozepur Cantt.

HERE is one *madariwala's* (magician) interesting introductory harangue used by a *madariwala* to attract an audience before he exhibited his magical prowess. He chose *Vanaspati ghee* as his theme: "*Bhaio aur behno*—we consider *Vanaspati* to be worthless. But let me tell you of its three great qualities: no thief breaks into the home of a *Vanaspati* user, no dog ever bites him, and he never grows old."

Having roused the audience's curiosity, the *madariwala* continued, "Why does no thief break into a *Vanaspati* user's home? Because he gets a bad throat and is kept awake all night by cough. No dog bites him because his vision gets blurred and he walks with the aid of a stick. And he does not get a chance of growing old because he dies young."

Contributed by K.L. Dutta, Dehra Dun

THE following ad appeared in a daily paper: "Are you illiterate? You don't know how to read or write? If so, do write to us and let us help you."

Contributed by J.P. Singh Kaka, New Delhi

A SARDARJI was boasting about the number of cities he had been to: London, Paris, New York, Rome, Karachi.

"You must know Geographia quite well", remarked one of his audience.

"Oh very well," replied the Sardarji, "I spent four days in Geographia."

Contributed by M.K. Dewan, New Delhi

A HARYANVI acquired a new Maruti, wangled a driving licence and took his car for an airing on the highway. He was not quite sure of the rule of the road and while driving on the wrong side collided with a car being driven by a young mod girl. Not much damage was done to the cars but the young lady was understandably furious. "You bloody fool," she screamed, "You think the road is your father's private property?"

Unabashed the Haryanvi replied in his rustic dialect, "Madamji, *mahrey baap kee to naheen, app kay pitaji kee sai; dahez main jald miljaigi*—it does not belong to my father but yours; however I hope to receive it in my bride's dowry."

Contributed by Shashank Shekhar, Meerut

A PUNJABI Romeo had been pursuing a girl who did not respond to his overtures. One day he had a big bump on his forehead. When his friends asked him what had happened, he replied, "My beloved not only threw a flower at me, she threw it with the flower pot—*Sajnaan ney phul maarya, par maarya gamley samet.*"

Contributed by Kanwarjit Nanda & Ranjit Grover, Mohali

W HAT do you call a very well-dressed man in Kerala?
—Debo Nair.

Contributed by Joydeep Ghosh, Calcutta

ANNE Landers' syndicated column is not famous for wit or humour; it is largely devoted to 'Dear Diary' kind of confessions and emotional yearnings. But this piece sent to me by Inder Gujral is truly hilarious. I reproduce it in total, in ignorance of copyright. In any event it is not Anne Landers' but one of her many readers who sent it to her. It is about problems that can arise if you give dog a bad name. This is how it goes:

"Everybody who has a dog calls him 'Rover' or 'Boy'. I call mine 'Sex'. He's a great pal but he has caused me a great deal of embarrassment.

"When I went to city hall to renew his dog licence, I told the clerk I would like a licence for Sex. He said 'I'd like one, too!' Then I said: 'But this is a dog.' He said he didn't care what she looked like. Then I said, 'You don't understand, I've had Sex since I was nine years old.' He winked and said, 'You must have been quite a kid.'

"When I got married and went on my honeymoon, I took the dog with me. I told the motel clerk that I wanted a room for my wife and me and a special room for Sex.

"He said: 'You don't need a special room. As long as you pay your bill we don't care what you do.' I said: 'Look, you don't seem to understand, Sex keeps me awake at night.' The clerk said: 'Funny, I have the same problem.'

"One day I entered Sex in a contest, but before the competition began, the dog ran away. Another contestant asked me why I was just standing there, looking disappointed. I told him I had planned to have Sex in the contest. He told me I should have sold my own tickets. 'But you don't understand,' I said, 'I had hoped to have Sex on TV.' He said: 'Now that cable is all over the place, it's no big deal anymore.'

"When my wife and I separated, we went to court to

fight for custody of the dog. I said: 'Your Honour, I had Sex before I was married.' The Judge said: 'The courtroom isn't a confessional. Stick to the case, please.'

"Then I told him that after I was married, Sex left me." He said: 'Me, too.'

"Last night Sex ran off again. I spent hours looking around town for him. A cop came over to me and asked: 'What are you doing in this alley at 4 o'clock in the morning?' I told him that I was looking for Sex. My case comes up Friday."

A PANDITJI and a Molvi sahib happened to be close neighbours in some posh locality of Delhi. Even though both were good friends, there was a certain amount of competition between them. If one had his drive done up, other had him relaid and so it went on.

One day the Panditji had a new custom built Cheverlett, so the Molana bought a Mercedes. When Molana looked out of his window it was to see the Panditji pouring water over the top of the car bonnet. He opened the window and shouted.

"That's not the way to fill the radiator, you know."

"Aha", said the Panditji, "I am christening it with Ganga jal, that's more than you can do to yours."

A little while later the Panditji was taken aback to see the Molvi sahib lying in the middle of road, hack-saw in hand, sawing the last inch of his car's exhaust pipe.

Contributed by Sushil Tikoo, Jammu Tawi

*I*N his introduction to *Fabulous Oriental Recipes*, Johna Blinn lists the following:

'Happy Home Recipe'

4 cups Love
2 cups Loyalty
5 quarts Faith
2 tablespoons Tenderness
1 cup Kindness
5 cups Understanding
3 cups Forgiveness
1 cup Friendship
5 teaspoons Hope
1 barrel Laughter

Take Love and Loyalty; mix thoroughly with Faith. Blend with Tenderness, Kindness, Understanding and Forgiveness. Add Friendship and Hope; Sprinkle abundantly with Laughter. Bake with Sunshine. Serve with generous helpings.

Contributed by Harprit Singh, New Delhi

A YOUNG lady still unfamiliar with the art of cycling ran her cycle into an old Sardarji's legs. The Sardarji turned round and asked angrily, "These are my legs, not a bicycle stand."

By sheer coincidence the next day it was the Sardarji who by accident ran his cycle into the young lady. It was the turn of the lady to reprimand him. "At your age and with your long beard, aren't you ashamed of coming on me on your cycle?"

"Bibi," replied the Sardarji, "my beard is not a brake."

Contributed by Harjeet Kaur, New Delhi

A PAKISTANI umpire raised his finger skyward as if signalling a batsman out lbw. The batsman remonstrated angrily "Why did you give the out signal when I am not out?"

The umpire replied coolly, "My dear fellow, I did not mean to signal out for you, I was only pointing to Allah who is merciful, beneficent and the final judge."

Contributed by Farhat Amin, Cuttack

T WO pandits riding on a scooter were stopped by a Punjab police constable. "Don't you know riding on the pillion is forbidden in the Punjab?" asked the constable, "I am going to challan you."

The pandits pleaded their innocence of rules but he refused to let them go. Very exasperated the pandit who was driving the scooter replied, "All right, *Ishwar* is with us. Do what you like."

"In that case, I'll challan you for having two on the pillion behind you."

Contributed by S.K. Bhalla, New Delhi

A N eight-year old sprained his ankle and was taken to hospital. The doctor took the child to the X-ray room where, seeing the large camera, it set up a howl of terror.

"We are only taking your photograph," assured the doctor. "Surely you have been photographed before."

"Yes," replied the child amidst his sobs. "Do I also have to smile for this one?"

Contributed by Reeten Ganguly, Tezpur

A PEASANT cycling along the road ran over a pedestrian. The pedestrian protested "*Kam say kam, ghantee to maar dettey*—you could have at least rung your bell."

The peasant replied—*ghanti kya? manney to cycle ka cycle maar daala*—what of the bell, I knocked the entire bicycle."

Contributed by Nav Jyoti, Batala

*T*HIS message written on the rear of a three-wheeler makes an interesting reading:

Aaj ki aawaz, hamen do bacchon peh naaz

(The call of the day, be proud of the two children you have)

But beneath the line was another:

Pappu, Pinki, Raju, Billoo tay Babloo di gaddi.

Contributed by Karan Dua, New Delhi

*B*ANTA Singh settled in England made friends with an Englishman named Lister, who became even more friendly with Banta's sister. One day Banta patted his friend and recited a couplet in English:

Lister, Lister,

I love your sister.

Lister was a little put out. Two days later, Lister retaliated by saying:

"Banta, Banta,

I love your sister."

"But that does not rhyme," protested Banta.

"No, it has no rhyme, but it has lots of reason," replied the Englishman.

Contributed by J.P. Singh Kaka, New Delhi

*T*HIS one illustrates the *nasbandi* theme. A teacher was examining her student's homework. The boys brought their exercise books in turns to be corrected. When the queue ended, the teacher called "*agla bacchaa—next child!*"

A boy shouted back "*abhi nahin—Not just yet!*"

Contributed by K.S. Bharadwaj

*I*N Swiss banks
We'll get our cuts.
In cannons and tanks
We'll empower.
Our Jack and Jill
There'll be no *buk buk*
Because of the Defamation Bill.

Contributed by Reeten Ganguly, Tezpur

A PASSENGER from Bombay on a visit to Singapore picked up uncomplimentary acronyms on the subcontinent's two major international carriers: Pakistan International Airways and Air-India.

P.I.A.: Please inform Allah.
A.I.: Already informed.

THIS anecdote is of Bihari-Bengali linguistic misunderstandings. It is about the spelling of the word ' assassination'. A boy who was having trouble remembering the sequence of letters was provided with the following formula in Bengali : *Gadhar upurey gadha, tar upurey ami, amar upurey nation* (an ass upon another ass, followed by me, followed by nation.)

Contributed by Dr. H.P. Sinha, Salempur, Chapra

LOOKING through the first Press Commission Report of 1954 presided over by Rajyadhaksha, I came upon a nugget. The commission was examining newspaper owners and questioning them about freedom given to editors. At the time Bennet Coleman (The Times of India group of publications) was owned by Seth Rama Krishna Dalmia whose grandson A.K. Jain presides over the newspaper empire today. Seth Dalmia maintained that he never interfered with his editors and as an example cited the campaign against prohibition carried out by the hard drinking editor of *The Times of India*,Frank Moraes. The commission was not impressed : "Why did you sack Feroze Chand?" a member asked Dalmia.

"Because he wrote bad English."

"Why did you sack Rana Jung Bahadur Singh?" asked another.

"For the same reason, his English was not good."

"Do you know the English language well? Do you regard yourself as an expert on the language?" asked the chairman.

"No," conceded Sethji naively.

ONCE I ran into V.N. Gadgil, MP (ex-minister of I & B) in an airport lounge. After some exchange of pleasantries the subject turned to the disastrous monsoon and what would happen if the drought continued. Gadgil promptly handed me the book he was reading and said, "This will interest you." It was a verse published in the *Sunday Times* (London) in 1978. Readers may find it amusing.

> Minister of Drought
> Began to go about
> Extolling every means of saving water;
> To husband what we had
> A garden rose was bad,
> Or flushing lavatories when we didn't oughter.
> "Let every flower die!"
> Became his battle cry.
> "Thrice use your washing water and suds."
> He kept this up for weeks
> Although a lot of Sikhs
> Prayed for rain precipitating floods.

"To err is human, to blame others for your errors is politics." This is an apt summary of an Indian politician's attitude to life. "Eat, drink and be heavy; for tomorrow you may die." In the event you may want to prolong your life as well as ensure your privacy, instead of consuming an apple every 24 hours, take my advice: "A raw onion a day, keeps everyone away."

Contributed by Kamaljit Singh Ahluwalia, Amritsar

A JOKE doing the rounds of Delhi's diplomatic cocktail circuit, though slightly over the line of propriety, deserves to be told because it llustrates the kind of feelings that obtain between Indians and Pakistanis. It is said that the President of the Soviet Union was celebrating his silver jubilee. As head of State he desired that all countries accredited to it should present him with the best of its products. First came the American ambassador with a brand new Cadillac. The President graciously accepted the gift. It was followed by the British ambassador presenting the latest model of a Roll's Royce. The President was delighted and desired that his thanks be conveyed to Queen Elizabeth II. The next was the ambassador of Israel. He had brought a new variety of elongated lemon developed in his country. The President was furious and ordered the lemon to be put up the Israeli's posterior. Then came the Indian ambassador. He presented a luscious Alphonso mango. The President was not amused and ordered the fruit to be stuffed up the Indian's behind Having been subjected to the painful insult the Israeli and the Indian ambassadors met in the lobby of the Kremlin Palace. The Israeli looked woebegone. The Indian was wreathed in smiles.

The Israeli asked the Indian, "How can you manage to look so happy after what has been done to you?"

The Indian ambassador replied, "You've no idea what is in store for the ambassador of Pakistan. He has brought the largest water-melon developed in his country."

A MINISTER due to go on a foreign tour had a lot of cash lying with him. He thought it would be safest left with the Prime Minister and requested him to keep it for him till he returned. The Prime Minister agreed but insisted that the transaction be witnessed by two of his senior assistants. "Money matters can lead to misunderstanding," said the PM. "It is always wise to have two witnesses."

The Minister saw the wisdom of the advice. The cash was handed over to the PM in the presence of two of his senior advisers.

Some weeks later when the Minister returned home, he called on the PM and asked for the return of the money.

"What money?" asked the PM "I don't know what you are talking about?"

"The cash I left with you," pleaded the Minister. "You even had two of your senior advisers as witnesses."

"Let's ask them," replied the PM. The senior advisers were sent for.

"Do you know anything about this Minister leaving money with me?" asked the PM.

"No sir, I know nothing," replied one. "No sir, he did not leave any money with you," said the other. The senior advisers left the room. The PM opened his safe and gave back the Minister his cash.

"Why did you first say you knew nothing about my money?" asked the bewildered Minister.

"I just wanted you to know what kind of advisers I have," replied the PM.

*T*HIS is an anecdote about a student looking for a textbook prescribed for his English examination. He could not recollect the title of the book. "I can tell you what the name of the book is in Hindi : *Maimney ki dum say hilti naashpaatee.*" The erudite bookstore owner was able to locate the required book : *Lamb's Tales of Shakespeare.*

Contributed by Shanti Swarup, Delhi

*W*HITE people have many unkind jokes about black and coloured emigrants. When colour of the skin does not lend itself to jesting, they find other unpleasant characteristics to jest about. Foreign emigrants in Germany are largely Turks who are as light-skinned as the Germans and are politely referred to as *gasterbeiters* (guest-workers). However, behind their backs, Germans have a lot of nasty things to say. Many anti-Turkish jokes are variations of Nazi anti-Semitic jokes. Here are a few examples :

Question : What is the difference between a Jew and a Turk?

Answer : The Jew has it behind him.

Question : How does a Turk commit suicide?

Answer : By smelling his armpit.

Question : What is the difference between a disaster and a catastrophe?

Answer : When a plane-load of Turkish guest-workers crashes, that's a disaster. When it lands safely in Frankfurt, that's a catastrophe.

Question : If a bomb fell on the Turkey. How many people would be killed?

Answer : Two. The rest of them live in Germany.

OF America's dozen Ivy League Universities, on top of the list come Yale and Harvard or perhaps Harvard followed by Yale. By and large America does not have an upper class accent distinct from that of commoners as is heard in England. The only exception is Harvard which has imbibed some of Boston's Brahmanical air of superiority by its distinct upper class speech. This one is told of a freshman who asked a senior student: "Can you tell me where the library is at?"

The senior snubbed him, "At Harvard, we never end a sentence with a preposition.".

The freshman had a second go: "Can you tell me where the library is at, you asshole?"

THIS is a variation of the Hindi couplet—'Kal karna tha so aaj kar'—what you had to do tomorrow, do today—to describe civil servants' attitude to work:

Jo aaj karna hai so kal kar
Jo kal karna tha so parson;
kisee baat ka fikr na kar
Naukaree abhee hai barson

(What you had to do today, put off till tomorrow. What was to be done tomorrow, to the day after; Let nothing bother you, have no fears, Your service is secure for many years.)

Contributed by Satendra Singh

TEACHER: "Like Satan you keep talking rubbish all the time! Do you ever take the name of the person who gave you birth?"

Student: "Whenever I try, I take the name of my mother. The fear of being ticked off by my father, makes me keep silent."

Teacher: "What does your father do?"

"Sir, exactly the same as you. He is forever rebuking me."

Contributed by Jawand Singh Bhatia, Chandigarh

HITLER and Mussolini after their death straight away go to hell. There they meet God. God asks them to come to his room one by one. First call is for Hitler, he goes inside. God asks him, "Hitler how many women you had, . . ." He replies, "Sir, one and only one."

God says, "Very good", and gifts him a Mercedes and tells him to have a nice time.

Now it's Mussolini's turn. He goes inside and was asked the same question. He replies, "Sir, six." God gets very annoyed and tells him, "Take this Ambassador."

After some time when Mussolini was taking a ride in his car, he hears Hitler laughing very loudly. He gets very angry, gets out of the car and asks Hitler "Why are you laughing at me?" He replies, "Mussolini I am not laughing at you. Just now I saw the Pope who whizz passed on skates!"

Contributed by Seema Maini, New Delhi

I WAS on a visit to Vijayawada and staying in a hotel which only served vegetarian food. One evening I wanted a change and asked the waiter where I could find a restaurant which served meat. "For that you have to go to a military hotel," replied the waiter.

I hired a three-wheeler to take him to the cantonment which was a long way away from my hotel. On my return I asked the hotel manager if there was nothing nearer than the cantonment for me to get a non-vegetarian meal. "You need not have gone to the cantonment at all," replied the manager. There are lots of restaurants nearby which would cater to your needs. In Vijayawada all hotels serving meat are known as Military Hotels."

Contributed by H.S. Dadyala, Guwahati

A DELHI official, a Bombay girl and a Mathura cow—all manage to get back to their base.

Contributed by Prof. Gurcharan Singh, Patiala

A MAN who had no telephone in his home went to the house of his next door neighbour who happened to be the director of a company. The neighbour happened to be away so the man asked his aged mother if he could make a call. "Surely," replied the old lady pointing to the telephone. "The director sahib has gone to his office but I know he would not mind your using the phone."

The man looked in his notebook but could not find the number he wanted. "Where is the directory?" he asked the lady. "Oh, the directory! She is taking her bath."

Contributed by R.P. Malik, Panch Kula

36

A CONSTABLE nabbed four boys and charged them for gambling in a public place. He asked the first, "What were you up to?"

"Nothing Sir," replied the boy. "I just happened to be passing this way."

"And you?" he asked the second boy.

"Sir, I was waiting for the bus."

The policeman turned to the third boy. "Sir, I don't even know how to play cards, how could I gamble on them?"

The constable let the boys go but caught the fourth boy who had the pack of cards with him. "Then it must be you who was gambling."

"No, Sir, there was no one I could gamble with," he replied.

Contributed by Shrutindher Paliwal, Jaipur

A YOUNGSTER rushed into a barber's shop and asked to be given a hair-cut and a shave immediately. "You wait your turn young man after the others waiting before you have been attended to. It will take an hour or two."

The young fellow simply ran out of the barber's shop. He came the next day, the day after and for many days following. Every time he was told to wait his turn, he fled. Not being able to contain his curiosity, the barber asked his assistant to follow the young man and find out where he came from and where he went after leaving his shop.

The assistant did so and reported back: "I don't know where the fellow comes from but as soon as you tell him you will be busy for the next hour or two, he runs to your home."

Contributed by Gurnej Singh, Jalandhar

A TOUGH Haryanvi peasant swaggered into a restaurant and ordered for empty tumbler and a lemon. He asked everyone to look as he squeezed the lemon into the glass with his powerful hands. "If anyone here can get as much out of a lemon as I have I will give him five rupees."

A thin, bespectacled clerk accepted the challenge. With his frail hands he got more juice out of the lemon than the Haryanvi. "Wonderful!" exclaimed the Chaudhary, handing over the fiver, "but tell me how did you manage to squeeze out more than I?"

"I am from the income tax department," replied the little fellow.

Contributed by Navin Sharma, Bareilly

A HUSBAND and wife were quarrelling. The wife got up in temper, stuffed a few saris in her bag and was marching out of the house when the husband yelled at her, "Where the hell do you think you are going?"

"I am going to hell," she hissed back.

"In that case don't forget to say my *namaskaar* to your parents and relatives."

Contributed by K.L. Dutta, Dehra Dun

A ONE *maatra* (accent) comment on the letter box of the Rajendra Nagar Post Office was spotted. The *maatra* 'oo' was added to the signboard reading *daak ghar* (post office) making it into *daakoo ghar*—den of robbers.

Contributed by Shyam Sunder Dutta, Lucknow

A YOUNG Pakistani civil servant had just got married. He was desperately trying to find somewhere to live. His mother advised him to go and see the *faqir* (holy man) as a last resort. And so he did.

"What I'm looking for is a small apartment, nothing too expensive, just three rooms, kitchen and bathroom, with a balcony and if possible a telephone and..."

"Very well", said the *faqir*. "Take this incense and burn it in a little blue teapot. A *djinn* will appear, who will make your wish come true."

The young man did as the *faqir* said. He burned the incense in a little blue teapot. And, sure enough, the *djinn* appeared.

"Your wish is my command!"

"Well, I'd like a small apartment, nothing too expensive, just three rooms, a kitchen and bathroom, with a balcony if possible a telephone...."

"Is that all?" the genie asked. "You fool! if I had a three-roomed apartment, do you think I'd be living in a teapot?"

*S*IKHS have a legitimate grievance against the media. Whenever a crime is committed and the wrongdoer happens to be Sikh, the press describes him as a Sikh thief, robber or killer. Have you ever read similar religious identification applied to Hindu, Muslim or Christian miscreants? This is done deliberately to defame the entire community, say some Sikhs, whereupon a wisecrack remarked: "*Sikh-kabaab* has become the favourite dish of the Indian media."

Contributed by Tushar Kumar, Najibabad

*T*WO wives were boasting of their husband's prowess at football. Said one, "Once my husband kicked the ball so high that it took four hours for it to fall back to the earth."

"What of that," retorted the other. "Once my husband kicked it so hard that it took it four days to return to earth. With it there was a note reading: If this ball is again kicked upto the moon, it will not be returned."

Contributed by Zorawar Singh, Kanpur

*L*ITTLE boy was asked by his teacher how one should address the Pope.

"Your Sanctity," he answered.

"And the Queen of England?"

"Your Majesty."

"Very good! And what about Ayatollah Khomeini of Iran?"

"Your Funda-mentality," the boy answered.

Contributed by Reeten Ganguly, Tezpur

*A*S the driver put his bus into gear and was about to release the clutch, a sweet voice from the rear shouted: *Driver Sahib, zara rukiye: kapde utaar leyney deejeeay*— Driver, please stop and let me take off my clothes." All eyes turned back to have a look. It was a *dhoban*— washerwoman, trying to get off with her bundle of washing.

Contributed by J.P. Singh Kaka, New Delhi

40

*T*HOMAS, an old Syrian Christian friend though a Keralite, spoke fluent Tamil and was somewhat of windbag. We decided to spend a week end at a hill resort. The clerk at reception desk of the hotel where we had booked ourselves asked us to fill in the register with our names, nationalities, dates of birth, last place of residence etc. I had no problem filling in what was required of him. When it came to Thomas' turn, he asked what the item home address meant. "The place where you were born and lived, sir," replied the clerk. Thomas confused the poor clerk with his biodata. "I was born in Cochin, brought up in Trivandrum; we moved to Ernakulam. I live in Madras but my real home is Vazhoor in Kerala. What shall I enter in the register?"

Not to be outdone, the clerk retorted "let's make it simple. If you were to die this minute, where would you wish to have your remains sent?"

"Oh that!" remarked Thomas triumphantly, "the Vale of Kashmir".

Contributed by Reeten Ganguly, Tezpur

*B*ANTA, an inhabitant of England, was on his way to visit his relatives in Punjab. At the airport, he was met by his Tamilian friend, Ranganathan, who persuaded him to spend a few days looking round the capital before going on to his village. Ranganathan first took him to the old planetarium: "This is Jantar Mantar, *teri vuma* (Tamil for 'you know'!)" It sounded very offensive in the ears of Banta. Next, they went to the Qutab Minar. Before Ranganathan could open his mouth, Banta told him, "This is the Qutab Minar—*tera baap.*"

Contributed by J.P. Singh Kaka, New Delhi

A NEWLY-employed villager was very weak in English. Once he asked his more educated neighbour to draft an application asking for casual leave for a day as he was down with fever.

The neighbour dictated the application in the following words: "Respected Sir—As I am suffering from fever, I may kindly be granted casual leave for today only."

He kept a copy of his application for subsequent use. Later, on the eve of his sister's marriage, he wrote an application on his own. It read as follows: "Respected Sir—As I am suffering from my sister's marriage tomorrow, kindly grant me casual leave for the next two days."

Contributed by Shashank Shekhar, Meerut

A CAR engaged for an election campaign broke down on the road. While the driver was tinkering with the engine, a rustic came along and asked if he could get a ride to his village which was a short distance away in the same direction. "No", replied the car owner, "this car is only meant to take Congress voters from their villages to the polling booth. You get to your village on foot and then I may give you lift."

The car drove away. The driver remarked to his boss, "Sir, I am sure from this man's village we will not get a single vote."

"That was the whole idea," replied the boss. "I don't want my party to win because it did not give me the ticket."

Contributed by R.R. Sagar, Muzaffarpur

*T*WO young ladies going along the road carrying *raakhis* for their brothers noticed two good-for-nothing lads walking behind them. They became some-what apprehensive of their intentions. Being *Raksha Bandhan* they turned round and accosted their pursuers.

"I'll tie a *raakhi* on your wrist and make you my brother," said one to one of the boys.

The other girl repeated the formula to the other boy. The boys tamely submitted to having coloured strings tied on their wrists. But continued to follow the girls. After a while one boy said loudly to his companion, "Why don't you marry my *raakhi* sister and I marry yours?"

Contributed by M.L. Kakar, New Delhi

*T*HIS anecdote is of a certain Mr. Aiyar who having qualified for the Indian Civil Service was doing his probation in England. At a formal dinner, as was his habit, he began to eat with his hands. "How disgusting!" remarked the *Mem Sahib* sitting next to him "How can you eat with those dirty hands?"

"Madam, I wash my hands before taking a meal," replied Mr. Aiyar. "Our knives, forks and spoons are sterilized after they are used," she maintained.

Not to be outdone, Mr. Aiyar replied: "That may be so Madam. But my hands and fingers go only into my mouth. Can you say how many mouths your knives, forks and spoons have gone into?"

Contributed by Mrs. Chitra Murthy, Jammu

A POPULAR heroine in the party with mark 'V' on her dress!

"What does that V mean?" asked one of her fans.

"V means virgin," she replied. "But, never mind, this is an old dress I am wearing today."

Contributed by Sudesh Kumar Wadhwa, New Delhi

*D*URING British Raj an English Colonel Commander of an Army Cantt in Madras joined a dinner hosted by the Jawans to celebrate a local festival. The menu was typically Madrasi.

Next morning at breakfast he commented to his wife, "Today I have discovered why the bloody Indians use water in lavatory; toilet paper could catch fire."

Contributed by M.K. Tulasian, Gorakhpur

*A*N old bishop in the nation's capital was sick to death of the socials and the embassy parties, he was to attend every other day. At one of them, he entered wearily, and sank into the nearest chair. The hostess asked coyly, "A pot of tea, bishop?"

"No tea," roared the bishop.

"A cup of coffee, My Lord?"

"No coffee," growled the bishop.

An understanding lady, she whispered in his ears, "Shall I serve you Scotch and water?"

"No water," said the bishop brightening.

Contributed by Judson K. Cornelius, Hyderabad

QUESTION: Why is a bad government like a bikini?
Answer: Because people wonder what's keeping it up.
And they wish it would come down.

Contributed by Annar and Vijay, Patiala

A FEW years back Bombayites were up in arms against the deteriorating civic amenities of the metropolis. The dug-up roads, mountains of refuse, open man-holes and unhealthy atmosphere in the civic hospitals caused public anger. The newspapers of Bombay also backed the citizens of Bombay and, day in and day out, articles were written about the utter lack of civic amenities inspite of the huge municipal taxes collected by the Corporation.

In this surcharged atmosphere, the cross road between Bandstand and Hill road was dug up to lay sewer drains of bigger dimensions—a routine matter for the BMC. The engineer-in-charge hit on an idea and instead of putting up that rickety board "CAUTION MEN AT WORK", he displayed a neat blackboard and wrote in bold letters "CITIZEN—YOUR TAXES ON WORK."

Next morning the engineer found himself oversmarted by some guy who had added one line to the idea: "GOING DOWN THE DRAIN."

CITIZENS
YOUR TAXES ON WORK
GOING DOWN THE DRAIN

Contributed by J.L. Manwati, Bombay

45

A HAWKER of sweets in Patna made good use of his name to sell his wares. He used to go round the streets shouting *Mathuraji kay peyday—pedas* of Mathura." Mathura being famous for its sweets, particularly its *pedas*, he did good business. One day he was asked: "Baba, how do you manage to bring *pedas* from Mathura every day?"

"I never said I brought them from Mathura," replied the hawker, "my name is Mathura Das."

Contributed by Sheshank Shekhar, New Delhi

A GOVERNMENT servant went to a doctor. "Doctor Sahib, I am suffering from exhaustion. Please advise me."

The doctor examined him carefully before replying. "What you need is complete rest. You should return to the office as soon as you can."

Contributed by J.P. Singh Kaka, New Delhi

A DONKEY was in the witness box. The cross-examining lawyer addressing the court said, "Your Honour, this *gadha*......" The witness shouted, "Your Honour, I object to the insinuation."

The judge said—"But aren't you one?" The witness clarified, "It is not the word that matters. It is the manner in which the word is uttered and the meaning sought to be conveyed that matters."

The judge ruled—"Objection sustained."

Contributed by R.N. Patro, New Delhi

*I*T was my first visit to Chhattisgarh and tried to show off my knowledge of plants to my Chhattisgarhi guide and mentor, Shyam Lal Chaturvedi. He listened with rapt attention while chewing *paan*. I point to the ipomoea and tell him that although it is a noxious weed, since it is in flower all the year round, Guru Gobind Singh gave it the name *Sadaa Suhaagan*—ever in marital bliss. Chaturvedi spits out betel juice and tells me that Chhattisgarhis have a more appropriate name for it. "It grows everywhere where there is garbage. You cut it down to the roots and it sprouts again. You stick a branch of it in the dust and it becomes a bush. There is no way you can get rid of it. In Hindi they call it *be-sharm*—without any shame. Chhattisgarhis have coined a better name for the pestilential weed: we call it *paaliteeshan* (politician)."

*A*NGRY repartee between quarrelling husbands and their wives has contributed richly to our corpus of humour. The following exchange is reported to have taken place between a couple. An irate wife yelled at her husband: "You are a very stupid man. Your brain is just full of *bhoosa*."

The husband shot back, "Now I know why you keep eating my brain (*dimmagh khatee ho*). That is because you are a *gadhee*—a she-donkey."

*T*EACHER of a senior class of a co-ed school: "Can anyone define what the term classmate means?"

Bright student: "Yes sir, students who mate with each other in classrooms are known as classmates."

Contributed by Neeraj Talwar, Dehra Dun

ONCE upon a time there was a rich *zamindar* who liked to end his day by taking a bowl of whipped cream *malaee* before retiring for the night. He had a servant whose job was to get three *annas'* worth of *malaee* from a *halwaae* every evening. He became suspicious of this servant's honesty and engaged another to keep a watch over the fellow. The two servants came to an understanding. Instead of buying two *annas'* worth and pocketing one *anna,* they began to buy one *anna's* worth for their master and dividing the other two between themselves.

After some days the *zamindar* smelt collusion and hired a third servant to keep a watch on the other two. This time the three of them came to an understanding whereby they divided the three *annas* between themselves. At night they smeared their master's moustache with white paint. Next morning the *zamindar* spoke angrily to his servants, "I got no *malaee* last night. Why?" The servants protested that he had and showed him a mirror which showed the white on his moustache.

The gist of the episode can be concluded thus.

In the first decade of Independence only 25 per cent of India was corrupt; in the second, 50 per cent; in the third, 75 per cent and in the fourth, 100 per cent. Now we enter the decade when a white smear on the moustache fools the people that they have had their dessert.

Contributed by K.K. Aggarwal, Ghaziabad.

CHANGE in Rashtrapati Bhawan :
Goodbye and farewell to *tandoori* chicken,
From now *idli-sambhar* will rule the kitchen.

Contributed by Reetan Ganguly, Tezpur

*T*HIS is an example of a literal translation of Hindi into English. One teacher, while talking to his colleague, was interrupted by a student. The teacher ticked off the student in the following words: "When I talk and he talk, don't come in between."

On another occasion, the same teacher reprimanded a student who was tardy in attending classes: "A day late, two days late, daily daily late, I cannot late rate."

Contributed by Dr. R.R.S. Rathore, Pant Nagar

*I*N a Test match every decision of the umpire was received by the spectators with hoots of derision. The umpire finally decided to quit the field and joined the crowd. A spectator asked him. "Why are you sitting here?"

"I am trying to find out if I can see the game better from here and give the right decisions." replied the umpire.

Contributed by Syed Moin Munawar, Hyderabad

*D*URING his stay in Sohna, Haryana, the Opposition leader felt he needed a haircut and sent for a local barber. At the end of the operation, the barber demanded a price double that of the usual charge. "I have so little hair on my head," complained Raja Sahib. "Why are you charging so much?"

The Haryanvi *nai* replied: *"Double charge kaatnay ka na laiven baal dhoondhna ka leiven sai* (I am not charging you double for cutting but looking for your hair)."

Contributed by Shashank Shekhar, Meerut

A SUPERINTENDING Engineer (S.E.) of the CPWD was inspecting the furniture section. He wanted to test the knowledge of his subordinates.

"What kind of wood is this?" he asked one.

"Teak, sir. C.P. Teak," replied the subordinate.

"And the plywood?"

"Duroply sir. It bears the ISI mark. Best in the market.

"And the board?"

"Pamella Borde, sir," replied the smarty subordinate.

"What do you mean? This is Duro board," growled the S.E.

"Sir, we have renamed it Pamella Borde, because it is the best available and universally used."

Contributed by Inder Dutt Salwad, New Delhi

*D*URING the days of the Raj, on a Christmas eve, a profoundly pro-British Khan Sahib went over to the bungalow of the Deputy Commissioner (who happened to be a Britisher) with a basketful of luscious fruit. Being illiterate, the Khan Sahib conveyed in his Punjabi dialect his good wishes to the Sahib for X-mas and the New Year, saying.

"Hazur Lambi Umar Payen"

The Sahib in broken Hindustani returned the compliment thus,

"Tum Sala Mat Raho".

The redoubtable Khan Sahib left in a huff and soon joined the Freedom Party.

Contributed by R.R. Sagar, Muzzaffarnagar.

A MAN who had more beer than was good for him staggered into his house and rushed to what he thought was his bathroom to empty his bladder. Having relieved himself of his burden, he confronted his wife, "There must be a ghost in the bathroom," he stuttered. "I opened the door and the light went on; I shut it and it switched off on its own."

"It wasn't the bathroom door you opened," replied the wife very icily, "it was the refrigerator."

Contributed by M.S. Vali, Hyderabad

*H*ERE is a variation of the one-legged *tandoori* chicken anecdote. A *dhabawala* who had been questioned for serving such a bird took his customer outside and showed him a hen which happened at the time to be standing on one leg. The customer cried "shoo, shoo". The hen promptly scampered away on its two legs. Unabshed the *dhabawala* replied, "Sir, if only you had shouted 'shoo shoo' before eating my chicken, the second leg would have appeared."

Contributed by Rekha Gupta, New Delhi

*B*ANTA Singh, like all good Sardars, always greeted everyone in the congregation with a loud. *"Wahey Guru Ji Ka Khalsa, Wahey Guru Ji Ki Fateh."* After spending a few years in England he returned home and at the village gurudwara produced an Anglicised version of the greeting: "Sat Sri Akal. And a copy to all."

Contributed by J.P. Singh Kaka, New Delhi.

My friend Onkar Singh who returned from Ahmedabad last week posed a question which I could not answer. "How is it that in Gujarat where every man is a *bhai* and every woman a *ben* and population keeps on increasing?"

J.P. Singh Kaka has drawn my attention to the same kind of confusion that exists in the minds of some people. A bachelor on the look-out for a wife was advised by a friend to put in an ad in the matrimonial columns. He took the advice. A few weeks later his friends asked him if he had any luck. "Yes," replied the bachelor and added naively, "*kaee bahnon kay to khat bhee aaye hain*—many sisters have written to me."

ONE day a *bania* boy quarrelled with his *jat* friend and called him *bewakoof jat*—stupid peasant. The *jat* rewarded him with a light slap across the face. The boy went and complained to his father.

"You deserved what you got," reprimanded the father, "When you called him a *jat* you did not have to add *bewakoof* to it."

Contributed by Ram Singh Suhag, Hissar

SHORTLY after her husband's death, the widow married her husband's brother. Hoping to avert small-town criticism of such a hasty marriage, she hung a huge portrait of her late husband in the living room.

One day a visitor asked about the fine-looking man in the portrait. Dabbing away a tear with a hankie, she answered, "That's my poor brother-in-law. He died recently."

A TEACHER asked class six to write a short composition entitled "Flowers". One of the essays submitted read as follows: "Some men favour flowers. They even wear them in the bottom holes."

Contributed by Wilfrid Singh, Darjeeling

A HARYANVI peasant being taken ill came to Delhi and was admitted to the All India Institute of Medical Sciences. Internee medical students came round in turns to examine him. Being Bengalis, Tamils and Punjabis none of them could understand what the ailing Haryanvi was saying to them in his dialect. Ultimately a Haryanvi lad working as a compounder in the hospital pharmacy came in, and asked, *"Taoo, tainey kay ho gaya* (Uncle what's gone wrong with you)?"

The peasant beamed: *"Rey chhoray, daktar to too sey, bakee to sab kampoder laagain sey* (O boy, you must be the real doctor, those others appear to be compounders)."

My FRIEND Lakhan Naqvi told me of a dream he had some months ago of my dying and resurrection. I was so tickled by it as a kind of summary of my life that I thought of sharing it with my readers.

The wire services reported that I was seriously ill. (I doubt if my illness will merit reportage from either PTI or UNI). The next morning he read that I had proceeded towards my 'heavenly abode'. He decided to call and condole with my family. He saw me laid out in a coffin. As he came to put some flowers on my corpse, I said, "Lakhan, get me a bottle of Scotch."

Lakhan was startled and replied "You are supposed to be dead. You are not meant to talk after you die."

I replied, "Some lazy people go dumb when they die. Active people like me can go on talking till they are cremated. Get me a bottle of Scotch."

Lakhan, being a good boy, dutifully got a bottle of Scotch and placed it by my side.

I was taken to the crematorium. As the mourners were returning to their homes, Lakhan, who was by then in his car, saw me coming out of the cremation ground. He opened the door of his car to let me in. "What happened?" he asked somewhat stupefied. "How did you manage to survive the cremation?"

"I bribed Yama with the bottle of Scotch you gave me. He let me return to the world. Take me back home," I replied.

TEACHER: "Who can tell me where we find mangoes?"

Hakim: "I guess everywhere womangoes."

Contributed by Hakim H. Nabijee, Bombay

A VEGETABLE seller's wife gave birth to a son. A customer who heard the good news, congratulated the greengrocer and enquired about the new born's state of health, *"Ji, ek dum taaza hai*—sir, it is absolutely fresh."

Contributed by J.P. Singh Kaka, New Delhi

*A*N assistant working with a foreign concern applied for a loan to buy a scooter as he had to travel more than thirty kilometres per day and change three buses to reach office. Management took a sympathetic view and sanctioned the loan for purchase of scooter on the condition that if the assistant failed to pay the monthly instalments to clear the loan, the scooter purchased would be impounded by the company.

The assistant then applied for a loan to build a house. The management again sanctioned the amount required with the condition that if he failed to pay back the amount in monthly instalments, his property would be impounded by the company.

Now that the assistant had a scooter and a newly constructed house, he felt he could take a wife and applied for another loan for marriage expenses. It was granted with similar condition that if he failed to pay monthly instalments, the goods acquired by the loan would be impounded by the company.

The assistant acquired a wife. The marriage did not turn out as well as he had hoped for because his wife constantly nagged him for money. The assistant found an easy way out of his predicament. He stopped paying the monthly instalments of the marriage loan.

Contributed by Rajan Bhatnagar, New Delhi

*B*ANTA SINGH, a Punjabi cobbler, found a job in a leather factory in England. It had all the modern gadgetry which got Banta very baffled. When it came to a massive machine, the supervisor explained to him: "This is the latest in leather technology. We put a buffalo in at one end and ready-made shoes come out of the other."

Not to be outdone, Banta Singh replied, "We in India have a better machine. We put in old shoes at one end and get a live buffalo out of the other."

"That's wonderful! exclaimed the English supervisor, "What happens to the laces?"

"They come out as the buffalo's tail."

Contributed by J.P. Singh Kaka, New Delhi

*S*ARDARNI Banta Singh was talking to her neighbour, Sardarni Santa Singh, across the balcony. *"Bhainjee,* how have you managed to break your husband's bad habit of coming home late every night?" asked Sardarni Santa Singh.

"Simple", replied Sardarni Banta Singh, "one night when my husband was very late, I shouted 'Is that you Inderjeet...?' Santa never stayed late after that."

Contributed by Shashank Shekhar, Meerut

"*W*HY are all Sikhs named Singh?" asked an Englishman of his friend Banta Singh.

"You see, it is like this," replied Banta Singh. "Just as you have kings in England, we have Singhs in India."

Contributed by J.P. Singh Kaka, New Delhi

*H*ERE is an amusing example of a bloomer made by makers of sign-posts. The Lucknow Municipality decided to change the name of Laxman Park to Mukharji Park in honour of a dignitary of that name. The task of making the new signboard was left to the CPWD. At the ceremonial opening of the park, the mayor unveiled the signboard. And behold! it read Murakhjee Park.

Contributed by Om Prakash Singh, Sindri

*S*ARDAR Tehl Singh, an emigrant in Canada earned enough money to buy himself a brand new car. He drove out of the sales depot with L Plate in the car. As the car zigzagged down the main highway, a traffic cop picked him up, "Why are you going from one side of the road to the other?" he demanded. "I am learning how to drive", replied Tehl Singh. "You have to have a driving teacher beside you, may I see your licence?"

Tehl Singh pulled out an envelop from his pocket and replied, "Here I am learning driving by correspondence."

Contributed by Shivtar Singh Dalla, Ludhiana

A NEIGHBOUR asked his friend the *haal-chaal* of his son. The father replied, "Thank You. He's Puppy." The neighbour was shocked and asked, "What! What do you mean?"

The father said, "Puppy is an acronym for Prosperous, Urban, Post-Independence, Punjabi, Youth."

Contributed by Som Nath, New Delhi

*W*E are familiar with the witticisms written behind trucks and three-wheelers. Variations on their themes make interesting reading. For instance, there is the common one: "If you can read this, UR2 close." Amusing variation can be: "If you can read this, you are evidently literate, Congrats!" There is another one often seen on the roads: "Dont't come close to me. I hardly know you." We can improve on it: "Don't come close to me—I got AIDS". I have seen this one on a three-wheeler: "When I grow up, I'm going to become a Rolls Royce." Having learnt something of the way Delhi's buses are driven, one can improve on it: "When I grow up, I am going to become a DTC bus." For "My other car is a Mercedez Benz." We can have it slightly different: "My other car was sold to buy this one." We can also convert. "Life begins at forty; so let's really live it up," to a warning against overspeeding. "Life begins at 40—fines begin at 50."

Contributed by Rajeshwari Singh, New Delhi

*T*HE following words of wisdom appear in Shri Amrit Lal's astrological column in Sunday of Feb. 12, 1989.

"A splendid opportunity will come your way this week... Problems may arise on the professional front so much so that you may even lose your job...."

Contributed by J.B. Mohapatra, Bhilai.

THiS is a true story of a correspondence which went awry because of a typing error. The stenographer working in the physics department of the university applied for one month's leave. The head of the department agreed, and asked him to type out an application to the registrar asking for a substitute. Instead of using the word substitute, the steno put in the word prostitute. The boss signed the letter without reading it.

The registrar, who had scores to settle with the head of the department of physics, "decided to cash in on the error. He wrote back: "Please refer to your letter Do... dated... The commodity asked for by you is not readily available in the store of the University. You are advised to procure it from the market and forward the bill to the Administrative Officer."

Another clerk applying for leave sent the following to his boss: "My wife is unwell. As I am the only husband in the house, kindly grant me leave for the day."

Contributed by Jasbir Singh Bindra, Ludhiana

A WOMAN sued her husband for deserting her. She had thirteen children aged 1 to 13. The judge asked her, "When did your husband desert you?" She replied, "Twelve years ago."

The judge was astounded. He asked, "Then how do you have all these children?"

The woman replied coyly. "Well, my husband kept coming back to say that he was sorry."

Contributed by Debesh Mukherjee, Dombivli

IN Bombay and Ahmedabad, one comes across many *Shahs*. Bombay Telephone Directory has longest list under the heading *Shah*. A full 32-page.

I was wondering afterall from where so many *Shahs* come till my doubt was cleared on seeing one big signboard in Prabhadevi area mentioning 'Shah Manufacturing Company.'

Contributed by Aditya Kiran Aggarwal, Pune

OUR professor asked us to define brain. My friend got up and replied, "Brain is what a man looks for in a woman after he has looked at everything else."

Contributed by Debesh Mukherjee, Dombivli

A CERTAIN Hindi zealot went to Pandit Harichand Akhtar and as if to help enlarge the latter's vocabulary, said, *"Hindi hamaare Bharat ki rashtra bhasha hai. Isliye, ab cycle rickshaw-puller ko tritiya chakra vahak kaha jayega."* (Hindi is the national language of Bharat. Therefore, now the cycle rickshaw-puller will be called *tritiya chakra vahak.*)

Pandit Akhtar drew a deep sigh and said, *"Kaam pahle hi se zaleel thha. Ab naam bhi zaleel hogaya."* (The profession of a rickshaw-puller was already undignified. Now the name also has become undignified.)

Contributed by Judson K. Cornelius, Hyderabad

61

A NEW visitor to a home asked a child, "*Beta* what is your name?"

"Uncle, my name is Pappu."

"That is surely your nickname; school *ka naam kya hai* (What is the name of your school)?"

"Salwan Public School," replied the child.

Contributed by J.P. Singh Kaka, New Delhi

T HIS one is a true experience of a Bengali friend living in a predominantly Punjabi colony of Shimla. One day when out shopping in the bazaar, he ran into his Punjabi neighbour, an elderly lady. As he greeted her, she responded with a smile, "I know I had forgotten to buy something for the family. Meeting you has reminded me what it was, *rasgullas.*"

Contributed by Reeten Ganguly, Tezpur

B ANTA SINGH happened to be in a queue at a railway station ticket counter with two men ahead of him.

"Ek Punjab Mail dena" (give me one for the Punjab Mail), demanded the man in front. He was given a ticket.

Then came the turn of Banta Singh, *"Ikk Punjab female dena."*

"What do you mean by Punjab female?" asked the clerk.

"It is for my wife," replied Banta Singh.

Contributed by J.P. Singh Kaka, New Delhi

A VERY brave Haryanvi who feared nothing was employed as a keeper of lions in a zoo. The lions held him in awe and respect. The only one the Haryanvi feared was his quarrelsome wife. If he was late returning home from the local *theka*, she gave him hell. One evening he was later than usual and rather than face his irate wife decided to spend the night with the lions. The wife looked for him everywhere she thought he might be. Finally she went to the zoo and found him fast asleep resting his head on the belly of the biggest lion. "You bloody coward!" She screamed, "*Vaisey to bahut bahadur bantai sai; aj deykh lee teyree bahaduri*" (You make yourself out to be such a brave man; today I've seen what a coward you can be.)

Contributed by Shashank Shankar, Meerut

W HAT do you call a man from Kerala, who picks up all the girls he wants to?
—Pheno Menon.

Contributed by Joydeep Ghosh, Calcutta

ONCE a violent quarrel broke out between husband and wife. The wife picked up her *belan* (rolling pin) and advanced menacingly towards her husband.

"Don't break the *belan*," pleaded the husband, "it costs money."

"It is my property and I'll do what I like with it," shrieked the wife.

The husband ran and hid under a charpoy. "Come out, you coward!" roared the wife, "You were so concerned about the *belan* which belongs to me."

"This house belongs to me," replied the husband, "I can hide wherever I like."

Contributed by Karan Dua, New Delhi

IT is sad to see the decline in the habit of reading. Rich Indians who can afford to buy books rarely have any in their homes. Their children spend hours stupidly gaping at their television sets. The blame must rest squarely on the shoulders of the parents. It reminds me of a dialogue between the mother and father of a child at school: "Our Bobby's teacher has written that Bobby should have an encyclopaedia."

"Encyclopaedia?" queried the father angrily, "Why can't he walk to school like the other boys do?"

GUJARATIS have problem pronouncing the word wrap and usually render it rape. Kannadigas go one better; they spell the word the way our gujju friends pronounce it. A Hari Prakash of Bangalore writes of an accountant of a local weekly who, when the publication was delayed, had to hire casual labour to wrap magazines in brown paper for posting. In the cash payment voucher he entered the explanation, "paid to casual labour towards raping charges." If the work load was heavy, the entry often read, "paid to casual labour towards raping through out the night."

A YOUNG Sardarji was lying under *peepal* tree enjoying the cool of the shade unconcerned with the turmoil of the world. A greybeard tried to persuade hime to be more aware of his duties to society: "You should be doing some work, not wasting your time relaxing under a tree," he said.

"What will I get by working?" asked the young man.

"Money."

"Then what?"

"With the money you can buy a house, marry a nice girl and have children."

"Then what?"

"Educate your children. Set them up in business."

"Then what?"

"You could have your savings, retire and relax."

"That's exactly what I am doing now, relaxing."

Contributed by Harjeet Kaur

RHYME without reason. It has always been a puzzle
to me...
What sailors sow, when they plough the sea;
What was it made the window blind?
Whose picture is put in frame of mind?
When a storm is brewing, what does it brew?
Does the foot of a mountain wear a shoe?
Can drink be got from a tap on the door?
How long does it take to hatch a plot?
Has a school of herring a tutor or not?

 Can you fasten a door with a lock of hair?
 Does a biting wind ever bite you, and where?
 And say—'I'll admit this is quite absurd.
 When you drop a remark, do you break your word?

So, if you try to understand English grammar, you're in
trouble. The double meaning of each word would, make
your mind boggle. No wonder, the English say,
'Exceptions prove the Rule', in fact, one has to bend the
mind, double to find any rule!

 Therefore, throw reasoning to winds; just speak as
they do Anyway, the English themselves don't speak
English as they should.

Contributed by Sheroo F. Capadia, Bombay

*P*ERHAPS, the drollest figure in the annals of American law was Judge Ben Lindsay. A woman who had worked for him and his wife as a servant for some years, came one day asking that the Judge might recommend her son for a job.

"Why, Maggie," said Judge Lindsay, "I had no idea you were married. You have never mentioned this lad of yours before."

"Well," the woman said, "I'm not married, that's true. But I haven't been entirely neglected."

Contributed by Judson K. Cornellius, Hyderabad

*B*ANTA Singh: "*Yaar* Santa, last year the name-plate outside your house read Santa Singh B.A. This year it reads Santa Singh M.A. when did you get your Masters degree?

Santa Singh: "You don't understand. Last year my wife died, I put B.A. to indicate Bachelor Again. Then I took a second wife, so M.A. is Married Again."

Contributed by J.P. Singh Kaka, New Delhi

A SARDARJI woke up one morning and told his wife that he had a terrible dream. "I dreamt that I had become a widower, a *randa*".

The Sardarni Sahiba retorted: "The Guru forbid! May you live long. Instead of making you a *randa*, let Him make me a *randee*—widow."

Contributed by R.S. Dutta, Chandigarh

68

I REPRODUCE Rajeshwari Singh's take off from Lewis Carroll's *Walrus and the Carpenter* without comment:

The time has come, the Opposition said
To talk of many things
Of guns and subs and kickback deals
And brothers of movie kings;
Why the PM's seat is boiling hot?
And who gave Win Chaddha wings?
"But wait," the ruling party cried
"Before we have our chat
Some of our states are out of food
And all are broke, quite flat
We have to send them assistance
They'll thank us much for that."
"A loaf of bread," the citizens said
"Is what we chiefly need
Dals and *Vanaspati* besides
Will be very good indeed
And if you give us all of these
We can begin to feed."

A HARYANVI peasant was given to gambling. Much as his wife nagged him into giving up the bad habit, she failed. Ultimately she decided to put down her foot. "As from today there will be no gambling in this house. Gambling is a sin," she announced. "How can it be a sin?" her husband protested. "Men have been gambling since the times of the Mahabharat. Nobody called them sinful."

"Okay, if you want to follow the heroes of the *Mahabharat*, I can do the same. Remember, Draupadi had five husbands."

Contributed by Shashank Shekhar, Meerut

PSYCHOLOGIST: A man who, when a good looking girl enters a room, watches everybody else.

College-professor: One who has been paid to talk in his student's sleep.

Compromise: Art of dividing a cake in such a way that everyone believes that he has got the biggest piece.

Father: A banker provided by nature.

Confirmed-bachelor: One who thinks that the only thoroughly justified marriage was the one that produced him.

Flatterer: One who feeds you with an empty spoon.

Contributed by Atul Kumar Jain, New Delhi

SREE Sree, a famous Telugu revolutionary poet, when asked by another poet whether he should put more 'sparkle of fire' in his poems. Sharp reply came: 'No, no, do the otherway. Put your poems in the fire.'

Contributed by V.C. Goud, New Delhi

THE other day, our Health Minister, while inaugurating a newly-constructed operation-theatre of an hospital, said "The construction of this operation-theatre is indeed a commendable achievement. It had become highly essential for the patients to have a theatre of their own for the sake of their entertainment."

Contributed by Shashank Shekhar, Meerut Cantt.

*B*ANTA Singh: "Santa, if a woman becomes a President in India, what will you call her in Hindi?"

Santa Singh: "Rashtrapati"

Banta Singh : "Wrong. She will be called Rashtrapatni."

Contributed by J.P. Singh Kaka, New Delhi

A SCHOOLTEACHER was very irritated by her boys who took more care of their looks and dress than their studies. She said in her most sarcastic tone, "To look at you even angels would blush with modesty; but when it comes to brains, even donkeys hide their horns."

A smarty replied, "Madamji, the good Lord gave us our faces; whatever comes out of our brains is gifted by you."

Contributed by Jawand Singh Bhatia, Chandigarh

A PROFESSOR was conducting practical test for medical students. There were five male students before him all of whom were duffers. The doctor kept a model of a woman's womb before them and asked them to identify the organ. He gave them a clue that it was not present in him or in either of the students. Then after some discussions a 'brilliant' student got up and replied, "Sir, that organ is a brain."

Contributed by Debesh Mukherjee, Dombivli

A MAN was taking out his young and pretty daughter for a stroll. Coming from the other side he met an old acquaintance he did not much care for. As they embraced each other, the other man said loudly enough for the girl to hear, "Where did you find this lovely treasure?"

"When the Lord gives, His bounty is without measure—*Chappar Phaar Kay Deta Hai.*"

A little later the girl asked her father, "*Pitaji*, why didn't you tell him that I was your daughter?"

"What harm did it do to you? And it must have burnt him up with envy."

Contributed by Banarsi Das Kaura, Bhadsian

A RICH businessman was telling friends his plans for his three unmarried daughters. "I've put aside Rs. 2,00,000 for Savita who's 22, a Rs. 4,00,000 dowry for Vinita, who's 27 and Rs. 8,00,000 for Namita who's 36."

"Sir," said an ambitious young bachelor, "do you have a daughter who's 50?"

Contributed by Reeten Ganguly, Tezpur

*A*N anti-smoking enthusiast addressed a person who had just lit a cigarette. "Do you realise that one-third of the smoke from your cigarette is inhaled by me?"

"Is that so?" replied the smoker. "Every cigarette costs me 60 paise. So you owe me 20 paise for this one."

Contributed by Manoj Datta, New Delhi

73

SHORTLY after Maharaja Ranjit Singh had consolidated his empire, a *mirasi* was sentenced to death for committing a heinous crime. As was the custom, he was paraded before the court. Whilst going round, the *mirasi* kept on muttering something and clicking his fingers.

Intrigued by this strange behaviour, Ranjit Singh ordered that the fellow be brought before him. When questioned about what he was mumbling, he replied in all humility—"Sarkar, I was saying that you do not look it but one can never be sure of it." The Maharaja demanded angrily: "What do you mean by these words?" "Sir", replied the *mirasi*, "when I was a small boy my parents consulted an astrologer who told them that I would be killed by a bastard. Now, Sarkar you do not look it but then one cannot be hundred percent sure, can one?"

The Maharaja directed that the s......o.....b.......be released forthwith and thereafter no person was to given the death penalty.

Contributed by Annar and Vijay, Patiala

A HARYANVI sipping tea found the taste very flat and asked his wife to put in some more sugar. "*Aji soogar to out of stock hai*", she replied in her best Haryanvi English.

Their son, who heard the dialogue, asked his father what "out of stock" mean . "*Beta*, when something is not present, we say it is out of stock."

A few days later a relative came to call. The head of the household was away in his fields. When asked where his father was, the little boy replied, "*Chacha, pitaji to out of stock hai.*"

Contributed by Shashank Shekhar, Meerut

74

*T*HE senior executive got a telephone call to clear a proposal from the PM's Secretariat. He told his private secretary to keep in touch with the concerned department and let him know when the file came up. Unfortunately, when the PS was on leave, the file was routinely cleared by the executive, noting "Not Approved".

The next day the PS came back from leave and saw that the proposal had not been approved. However, the orders were yet to be issued. He took the file to his senior executive and said, "Sir, this is the file for which you were rung up by the PM's Secretariat but you have written ' Not approved '. Instead of changing the whole office note, the senior executive simply added the 'E' to the word "Not," making it "Note Approved"

Contributed by Harish K. Monga, Ferozepur

*W*HEN the ludicrous charade of the Dandi Salt March was re-enacted, I was away in the States. I heard a lot of ill-tempered comment on the new breed of *Satyagrahis* who participated in it. Gandhiji would never have let them within range of his *lathi*. A Parsi industrialist of Bombay told me of his own experience. He went to Dandi to see the end of the Second Salt March. For old times sake he dressed himself in a *khadi kurta-pajama* and a Gandhi cap. The crowd wasn't sure who he was except that he looked vaguely familiar and since he was accompanied by a lot of hangers-on, was an important personage. *"Kaun chee,"* asked many Kathiawari peasants. Then one answered loudly enough for my Parsi friend to hear *"Sab soon badda chore chhe*—he is the biggest thief of all of them."

AN American friend resident in India vouches for the veracity of this story about the Queen of England's last visit to India. A wealthy but not too well-informed industrialist of Calcutta pestered the then British High Commission to be allowed to shake hands with the Queen. The High Commissioner gave in and arranged for the Marwari to present the Queen with a bouquet of roses on the strict understanding that while doing so he would keep his mouth shut. When the great moment came, the Marwari gentleman could not contain himself and having made his salutation and presented the roses said: "Welcome to India Queen Mary of England!"

The High Commissioner, red in the face, hissed: "Shut up! any way Queen Mary has been dead for many years."

Unabashed the Marwari replied, "I am sorry my memory failed me. I should have said Queen Victoria."

My American friend refuses to divulge the identity of the Marwari industrialist. Any guesses?

A DEVOUT Hindu having lost his father called a renowned Pandit to perform *shradh* for the soul of the departed. When it came to serving his meal, the man asked, "Panditji, is it true that whatever you eat will reach my father in heaven?"

"Certainly," assured the Panditji.

"Then I must serve you what my father liked most," He said. Whereupon he laid a bottle of Scotch and a *tandoori* chicken before the priest. "These were his favourite food and drink."

Contributed by S.K. Bhalla, New Delhi

A YOUNG widow decided to become a life insurance agent. Her first contact was a newly married young executive. Like a good insurance person she latched on to him and would not take no for an answer. In sheer exasperation the young man asked her to give him one good reason for him take out a policy on his life. The lady clinched the argument by citing her own example. "My husband insured himself for Rs 20,000. I had to wait for some years till he died to get this money. Who knows your wife may be luckier and get a much larger sum much sooner?"

Contributed by S.R. Laroiya, Noida

*G*ANGA Singh Dhillon and Dr. Jagjit Singh Chauhan were having a very high-powered meeting of their supporters to decide on the next step they should take to realise their dream of getting Khalistan. The "president" spoke first:

"We have issued Khalistani passports but no country is willing to recognise them. We have printed Khalistani currency notes; but no one is willing to give you anything for them. We have designed a Khalistani flag but no one is willing to fly it on his car or display it outside his house.... We must find an emblem for Khalistan which will become immediately acceptable and be liked by everyone."

The "Vice-President" spoke next: "Every country has its national bird. I think we should have one too. A bird everyone in Khalistan will cherish. Any suggestions?"

With one voice the audience acclaimed their national bird: *"Tandoori chicken."*

77

*T*HIS anecdote is about Salehbhoy Abdul Kader who was Mayor of Bombay and later Minister of Prohibition of Maharashtra in the 1970s. Salehbhoy, like other civilised people, liked his liquor. At a reception in his honour, in a club, Congressmen turned in great strength. While he joined them sipping aerated water, his security guard took his position at the club bar. Every few minutes he would go and change the glass in his master's hand. When the party was over, his host came to him and said: "Salehbhoy, what about a real drink now that these Congresswallahs have gone?"

"Thanks," replied Salehbhoy with a big grin. "I have had my quota of four large pegs served by my security man. My favourite brand is known as Kader-Cola."

Contributed by J. Manwati

*B*HAGWAT Jha Azad, former Chief Minister of Bihar, was trying to impose discipline and punctuality in government offices. He was up against the Bihari tradition of taking things easy. This is a popular saying about civil servants.

Baraa bajey tak late naheen Teen bajey baad bhent naheen (If he comes in by noon, he is not late. No interview after three—he's gone home).

Contributed by M.A. Menzin, Patna

A GENTLEMAN boarded a train. In the compartment he found a Haryanvi peasant with his family. Very politely he addressed his fellow-passenger:

"Chaudhury *Sahib*, where are you going?"

"Can't you see? I am going by train (*Deekhay nahi? gaadi mein jaoon hoon*)."

The gentleman tried to make his question simpler for the Jat. "Chaudhury *Sahib*, where is this train going to?"

"Fool! the train will go where the engine takes it to; it is not driven by bullocks! (*Bevakoof! gaadi vahaan jaavai, jahaan injun lay jaavai. Bailan seyatee to yoo chaalai nahin*)."

"Chaudhury *Sahib*, you are quite right. You are going by train, the train will go where its engine takes it to, but tell me where is the engine taking it to?"

The Chaudhury *Sahib* replied angrily, "You must be crazy! Engines do not travel by road. It will go as far as the rail lines take it. (*Bhor paagal; injun sadak pai nahin chaalai sai; jhaan tak lainai challiain gee, injun jaavaiga*)."

The gentleman patiently pursued his enquiry. "Chaudhury *Sahib*, you are right about going by train; the train going where the engine takes it and the engine will go where the rail lines take it to. But just tell me where the rail lines take it to?"

The Jat snapped back, "The more educated, the bigger the ass! The rail lines are stuck deep into the earth and stay where they are; anyone who does not know this simple thing is not fit to sit in a railway train (*Aur padhey-likhey niray gadhey! Rail kee lain aarey jammeen kain gaarh rakhee sai. Yoon aray kei aray rajengi, kahin nahin jaati; too gaddi main savaaree kaarnai kabil nahin hey!*)."

Contributed by Subash Tuteja, Fatehabad

CHANDRA Shekhar was trying to impress on H.N. Bahuguna the need to join hands to defeat the Congress(I). The argument got very heated and Bahuguna exploded: "Impossible! it is like trying to mate a horse with donkey."

"Why are you making me out to be a horse?" asked Chandra Shekhar.

Contributed by Shashank Shekhar, Meerut

"WHAT do you think was the major achievement of the Congress(I) in Bombay?" I asked a senior citizen when I was in the metropolis a day after the party had ended its confabulations.

"We saw the emergence of Indira Gandhi as the supreme teacher of the nation," he replied. "She sensed the mental limitations of her supporters and since few of them could memorise—much less understand—her 20-point programme, she compressed the 20 into one—they should work for her son Rajiv Gandhi."

AFTER the last summit meeting between Rajiv Gandhi and President Zia-ul-Haq, the two met privately for a friendly exchange of views. "What is your favourite hobby? Zia-ul-Haq asked Rajiv Gandhi.

"I collect jokes people tell about me," replied Rajiv. "And what is your favourite hobby, Mr. President?"

"I collect people who make jokes about me", replied Zia-ul-Haq.

THERE are two words of Yiddish for which I know no equivalents in other languages. The first is 'chutzpah' (pronounced Khootspah). According to Leo Rosten, author of *The Joys of Yiddish*, the word combines insolence, gall, audacity, brazen nerve, effrontery, guts, presumption plus arrogance. It is that quality enshrined in a man, who having murdered his father and mother, throws himself on the mercy of the court pleading he is an orphan. Men who have chutzpah have rhinoceros hides and are usually successful. Most of the politicians and businessmen have a powerful element of chutzpah in them. I came across a charming example of one many years ago in the home of Chaudhury Brahm Prakash, then Chief Minister of Delhi. It was at a tea-party he had given for MLAs and pressmen. A year earlier, he had celebrated his elevation to Chief Ministership by acquiring a second wife. She had a babe in arms. As we were about to leave, this lady came out of the house to bid us farewell. Most of the guests congratulated the hostess for having given the Chief Minister another son. One, who wanted to appear closer to the family than others, suddenly snatched the babe out of its mother's arms and proclaimed "*Hamaara aslee leader to yeh hai* (he is our real leader)." The frightened child began to whimper and urinated in the fellow's hands. Quite unabashed, the fellow added, "Now you see the proof that he regards me as best friend? He wouldn't urinate in everyone's hands, would he?" Under the patronage of the Chief Minister this fellow rose to be the wealthiest and the most successful land developer in the capital city.

Another example of chutzpah is of a young politician on the make. He made it to a state Vidhan Sabha and became a Minister. He also kept up with leaders of the Opposition in case. His Chief Minister reported his dubious loyalty to the Prime Minister and asked for permission to drop him from the Cabinet. The young man demanded and was granted an audience by the Prime Minister. There were over a dozen people waiting in the reception room for their turn to see the Prime Minister. As soon as Rajiv Gandhi entered the room, this young man leapt forward, whipped out a knife from his pocket and slashed his own arm. With the blood he put a *tikka* on the forehead of the PM. "This is to prove my loyalty; I do it by spilling my life blood," he proclaimed. That very afternoon he went over to the Opposition.

The second Yiddish word is 'yenta'. According to Rosten it is a coarse termagant and a gossip monger. In actual usage it is applied to loud, assertive females ever ready to pick up quarrels. You know the kind who no sooner anyone brushes past them will yell, "*Apney ghar mein maan-bhain naheen hai* (have you no mother or sister that you take liberties with me)?" Come to think of it, Punjabi has an exact equivalent in an untranslatable phrase, *phupphey kutten*—one prone to beating her flabby breasts. You know who I mean.

HERE is an ingenious explanation of the reason why our golden girl P.T. Usha came last in the Seoul Olympics. She spent some of her training time in Lucknow and picked up *Lakhnavi tehzeeb*—etiquette. As one competitor after another caught up with her, she let them pass with a polite *pehley app*—you go ahead.

Contributed by Ajay Saxena, New Delhi

I CAME across the report of an amusing case in Israel which could very well apply to conditions obtaining in India today. Ten years ago a certain Billitzer borrowed £20 from Ephraim promising to return the loan next day. He didn't and asked for a week's grace. After a week Ephraim called on him and got a promise that the money would be returned the following Monday. It wasn't Ephraim engaged a solicitor who served Billitzer with a legal notice stating, 'Due steps will be taken in default of claim being met within a period of 72 hours.'

Two months passed without anything happening. Ephraim went to a better solicitor who filed a suit for the recovery of the loan. After five months the case came up for hearing. Billitzer put in a medical certificate saying he was ill. The case was adjourned for hearing a year later. On that date, Billitzer had gone abroad—and stayed abroad for another year and a half.

Ephraim engaged a leading solicitor to take up the case. The magistrate refused to take up the case in the absence of the defendant. Ephraim appealed to a higher court. This court rejected the appeal as it did not take cognizance of cases involving less than £50. When Billitzer came back Ephraim sent him another £30 through a notary to raise the debt to £50. The higher court sent the case back to the lower court with instructions to proceed with the case in the absence of the defendant. Billitzer returned and raised technical objections. Ephraim went to the Supreme Court and petitioned to the Minister of Justice. The Minister advised him to engage the best lawyer in Israel and get his advice. Israel's leading lawyer patiently listened to Ephraim's tale of woe and advised him to go to Billitzer's office and beat him up. This is precisely what Ephraim did. And got his £50 back.

Moral: It pays to consult a really good lawyer, and with his blessings, take the law into your own hands.

A VISITOR to the capital approached a man at a bus stand and asked. "Sir, will this bus go to Connaught Place?"

"Ya," replied the man.

Not understanding what the word meant he asked another who likewise replied. "Ya." So did the third and the fourth man. Then he approached a Sardarji and asked the same question. He replied, "Yes, sir it does."

The visitor further asked, "What does Ya mean? Why did you reply yes sir?"

"Sir ji, an educated, person always says yes sir. Only uneducated say ya," replied the Sardarji.

"Are you an educated person?"

"Ya."

Contributed by Poonam Mehta, New Delhi

*G*ORKHAS are famous for discipline they observe in the army and the respect with which they treat their officers. Once there was a fire in a highrise building occupied by the Army. No sooner they heard the alarm, a batch of Gorkha Jawans ran out with a heavy net to rescue those who jumped down from the upper storeys. Some clerks came down and were saved. Then their Commanding Officer leapt from the top floor. The soldiers saw him hurtling down. They dropped the net, sprang to attention and saluted. The Colonel was not as lucky as the clerks.

Contributed by M.L. Batra, Karnal

I HAVE carried anecdotes illustrating Maulana Mohammed Ali's ready wit. His younger brother Shaukat Ali was an equally witty person who, because of his enormous size was known as "big brother." There was a third and oldest brother, Zulfiqar Ali. Mohammed and Zulfiqar were minor poets. The muse of poetry had not affected Shaukat. A friend tried to needle him. "Your eldest brother Zulfiqar wrote verses under the pseudonym *Gauhar* (diamond); the next Mohammed wrote verses under the pseudonym *Jauhar* (jewel); what *takhallus* (poet pseudonym) do you use?

Maulana Shaukat Ali replied promptly, "My pen-name is *Shauhar* (husband).

Contributed by Jalal Zakaria

A CERTAIN gentleman was so busy making money that everytime anyone wanted to speak to him on anything except business, he replied : "I have no time." It became his *takia kallam* —a pillow word. His neighbours noticed that no sooner he left for his office, a young man came to call on his wife. The neighbours tried to warn him, but he brushed them aside with his pet phrase, "I have no time."

Then the neighbours decided to visit him together and tell him what was going on behind his back. "No sooner you are out of the house, this fellow comes in to have a good time with your wife."

"That is because I have no time." he replied.

Contributed by Harjeet Kaur, New Delhi

QUESTION: "Why do Indian men make such lousy lovers?"

Answer: "They get all the love they want from their mothers and by the time they attain puberty they become emotionally impotent."

EVERY time I go to Pakistan I pick up some jokes about its head of state most of them about his uncanny ability to outlast political opponents and his sense of public relations. Zia is an Arain—a caste of market gardeners who grow vegetables. It is said that having retired from his onerous duties, Zia was looking for something to do which would add to his pension. An old friend who knew Zia was an Arain, suggested that since he owned a lot of land they would go into growing vegetables on a 50-50 basis. "You do the work; what grows above the ground is yours, what grows below will be mine!"

Zia readily agreed and planted seeds of potatoes, radishes, carrots. He got the sale price of the entire crop.

His partner felt chagrined. "Next crop, I take all that grows below the ground and you take what grows above it."

Zia agreed. This time he planted cauliflowers, cucumbers, peas. Once more he got all the proceeds of the sale.

Time came for the third planting. This time the landowner was determined not to lose in the bargain. "Whatever grows below the earth and above it is mine; only the middle portion will be yours."

Zia agreed. And this time he planted sugarcane. The roots below and leaves on top went to the landowner; the middle portion which has all the juice fell to Zia's share.

TELEGRAMS were sent out inviting members of the party to attend the Congress centenary celebrations in Delhi. Some telegraph clerks not familiar with the English language changed the word centenary to sanitary. Another variation of the word was used by Prakash Patil, son of Vasantdada Patil, then the Chief Minister of Maharashtra. When questioned whether his father had really met Prime Minister Rajiv Gandhi, he replied in the affirmative: "Yes, at the century celebrations."

Then there was a member of Parliament who having spoken on the budget was correcting the transcript of his speech taken down verbatim. He lost his temper and exploded: "These fellows who prepare our Hansard get simple words wrong. I was talking on the baajet and they have taken it down as budget, not once but every time."

A MATERNITY home housed in the first floor of a multi-storeyed building had on the ground floor a dry-cleaner boasting of one-day service. Came a terrible dust storm which knocked down the maternity home's signboard. It fell on the dry-cleaner's obliterating all of it except the bottom line. After the storm had blown over the two signboards read collectively as follows:

Mamta Maternity Home. Delivery within 24 hours.

Contributed by Navin Sharma, Nainital

YOU have to be a master of words to mix flattery with satire. Our ancestors knew the art better than we. Badauni in his *Mantakhab* records some incidents when recipients of rewards were able to combine their disappointment with the gift with flattery for the emperor in the hope of receiving more. One was Mir Mahmud Mahwi who was presented with a horse by emperor Humayun. The disappointed civil servant addressed Humayun: "Exalted emperor who has an army like the great Jamshed's has given me a horse which is both lean and unsteady on his legs. When I mount it, after every two or three steps, it stumbles and says, 'now you carry me for the next two or three steps'."

Then there was the poet Anwari who was presented with an old horse which gave up the ghost on the very night it had been delivered at Anwari's home. Next morning the poet came to court on foot. "What happened to the horse we presented you yesterday?" asked the emperor.

Replied the poet: "It was so fleet-footed that in one night it traversed the distance from the earth to heaven."

A DEPUTATION of government servants met the Prime Minister and related their woes of stagnating in their jobs. The Prime Minister heard them patiently as is his wont and replied calmly, "I don't mind being the Prime Minister all my life without asking for even one single promotion. I don't understand why can't you be content with being LDCs, UDCs or Assistants."

Contributed by R.B. Kaplish, New Delhi

*T*HIS story is told about a young Sikh officer known for his ready wit. Soon after joining service in the mid-thirties, he had to go to Shimla on official work. At Kalka he boarded the narrow gauge train and found that his only companions were two middle-aged English ladies. They considered it infra dig to talk to an Indian. The young man felt isolated and whiled away his time by leafing through magazines.

There are 103 tunnels on the Kalka-Shimla railway line and the longest is that between Solan and Barog. It took nearly five minutes for the train to go through it. When it entered that tunnel, the lights somehow went off. An idea flashed across the young man's mind. Without getting up from his seat, he gave a resounding kiss on the back of his hand. After about 30 seconds, he repeated the kiss. A couple of minutes later, the train was out of the tunnel and natural light poured in. The two women looked at him and each other with daggers in their eyes. The young man watched the scene with a sly smile and got down at the next station, leaving it to the two woman to settle the matter between themselves.

Contributed by P.S. Chawla, Chandigarh

A DEVOUT old Christian lay on his death bed. Instead of a priest, he summoned his lawyer and his doctor and asked them to stand on either side of his bed. "Why do you want us beside you at this time?" they asked. Replied the dying man: "I want to die like Jesus Christ on the Cross with two thieves on either side."

Contributed by M.K.S. Panicker, Cochin

*I*N one of my columns on Afghanistan I quoted my photographer friend , the late Mr. Sharma, about the three categories of breaking wind. Reader Rajeshwari Singh of New Delhi has written to say that according to ancient texts there are four:

Uttamen dhamdhama
Taraturi chamdhama
Padhanaam phushkari rani
Tasya ghinaat na jaye

(Best is the loudest one. Second is the half-hearted attempt. Third is the slow whispering wind. Worst is the silent one whose stink doesn't go away).

My apologies to readers who restrict themselves to only three categories.

*A*S an income-tax officer (in-charge of administration) in Calcutta he often faced the problem of late attendance of staff. With a view to find out the reason, he added a column in the attendance register: "Reason for late arrival". It did not improve matters. The staff got into the habit of inventing excuses for coming late. If the first late-comer entered against his name, "Delayed due to late arrival of local train or traffic jam", other late-comers simply wrote 'Ditto' against their names. One day a lady stenographer arrived late by 20 minutes and wrote, "Went to consult lady doctor for maternity problems." Other persons who came late that day put down 'Ditto', 'Ditto'...

Contributed by R.N. Lakhotia, New Delhi

DESPITE censorship of the Press, a great deal of anti-government and anti-*Mulla* writing appears in Pakistani papers. The best-known exponent of modernism is Jammu-born Khalid Hassan currently living in Vienna. Compilations of his articles make very good reading. They are loaded with sarcasm and written in excellent English. In one he narrates the story of a *Maulvi* of Jammu delivering a sermon after Friday prayers. Far from felicitating them for being regular at their prayers, he thundered: "Those of you who are lecherously dreaming of spending your next life in the arms of *houris*, would do well to remember that it is your own wives who will catch-up with you in paradise."

The announcement was received with dismay. Then one out of the congregation named Allah Ditta spoke up: "*Maulvi Sahib*, if what you say is true, I wish to announce that I am going to join the *Arya Samaj* as soon as I get out of this mosque."

Allah Ditta's wife was the ugliest woman in Jammu.

A PRIVATE sector company invited applications for a post. Its advertisement specified that the candidate who spoke the least would be selected. The first applicant was a well-bred young man. His name was called. He opened the door and asked "*Andar pravesh kar sakta hoon*—Can I enter?" He was rejected.

The next one, brought up on Lucknawi etiquette, opened the door and asked: "*Ijazat hai?*"—Have I your permission?"

He was rejected for using more than one word.

The third was a Punjabi. As he opened the door, he used one word "*Varhan*—enter?" He was hired.

*T*RUST a lawyer to tell a joke against his own profession. Jasbir Singh Bindra, advocate of Ludhiana, has this about two pick-pockets outside a *theka*. After they had ordered their drinks, they saw a car pull up in front of a house on the other side and a fat *sethji* step out of it. Said one pick-pocket to the other: "Looks like a nice *shikar*. Let's polish him off before we enjoy our drink."

"Don't be silly," replied the other. "He has gone into the house of a lawyer. When he comes out, his pocket will have already been picked by his host."

*A*N INGENEOUS explanation based on philological analysis for the high death toll on Indian roads. Put forward like this: there is a popular two-wheeler on our roads called Yamaha which is similar to the *stuti* of our Hindu God of death *Yama* (pronounced Yamah). There is another vehicle names Matador which literally means a murderer or a killer. He is not a bull-fighter who is a to-read or from the Latin Taurus for bull. So there are two identified killers, Yamaha and Matador on our highways.

Contributed by Dr. Asoke Bagchi, Calcutta

A PERSON, looking for a house, contacted a property dealer. The only house available at a reasonable rent was known as *'Bhoot Bangla'*. The man got the address, proceeded to the house and rang the bell. Two men came out. The househunter asked, "Sir, is it true that this house is haunted?" The two persons looked at each other and replied: "You better ask someone living nearby; we died more than 50 years ago."

Contributed by Jasbir Singh Saharan, New Delhi

A SARDARJI farmer had saved up a lot of money to buy a car. But when he had the required sum, instead of buying a car he bought a buffalo. "Sardarji, you were always saying you wanted a car to drive to the *mandi*. And now you have gone and bought another buffalo. Won't you look ridiculous riding a buffalo to the market?"

Quite unabashed, the Sardarji replied, "Wouldn't I look more ridiculous trying to milk a Maruti?"

A BIOLOGY teacher was dissecting a frog. Having explained the inner features of amphibians, he asked his students, "What would you expect to find if you dissected a human being?"

A bright lad replied, "Sir, I would expect to find myself behind the bars."

Contributed by K.S. Bharadwaj

A VISITOR having tea at a restaurant complained about the quality of the tea.

"Sahib, we have got this tea from Darjeeling," explained the waiter.

"Is that why it is so cold?" asked the customer.

Contributed by J.P. Singh Kaka, New Delhi

A DHOBI won the first prize in a lottery and bought himself a small, electrically run laundrette. Since he had spent his entire winnings on the machine, he retained his donkey for collecting and delivering clothes. Unfortunately, due to some fault in his meter, the dhobi's first electricity bill was so large that he had to sell his donkey to pay it.

A short while afterwards, someone asked the donkey as to who was responsible for his master-of-many-years selling him. The donkey replied, in a loud, angry bray: "DESU! DESU! DESU! "

Contributed by Rajeshwari Singh, New Delhi

A SARDARJI, who was a prominent businessman of his town, lost his wife and the funeral became a public occasion. All the dignitaries of the town attended, and almost all were known to the bereaved sardarji. There was, however, a stranger and he seemed more upset than anyone else. Before the funeral was over, he broke down completely. The sardarji asked who was this weeping stranger. "Oh!" whispered someone, "Didn't you know. He was your late wife's lover!"

The widower sardarji moved across to the sobbing man, patted him on the back and said, "Cheer up young man, cheer up, don't lose heart for I shall probably marry again."

Contributed by Shashank Shekhar

A MUSLIM couple arrived in paradise and approached *Allah* for permission to have another *nikah* performed. *Allah* asked him to wait for some time. After waiting for some years, they again approached the Almighty with their request. *Allah* took them to his office and showed them a pile of thousands of pending applications asking for permission for a repeat marriage. "You see I can do nothing till some Mullah is allowed to enter paradise; there hasn't been one for many decades."

Contributed by Prof. Gurcharan Singh, Patiala

A BANIA shopkeeper died and was presented before Dharamraj. His account was examined and found perfectly balanced: he had as many good deeds to his credit as bad deeds on the debit side. After much thinking on the subject, Dharamraj left the option of going to *swarg* (heaven) or *narak* (hell) to the bania.

Without any hesitation bania replied, "You send me to any place where I can make a reasonable profit."

Contributed by Arun Baxi, Jalandhar

A RUSTIC was elected as the secretary of the association of the colony. He called a meeting at his house. After the meeting was over, someone asked him, "How did the meeting go?"

"Oh, it was very sexful," replied the rustic.

"Surely, you mean successful," his friend queried.

"What is the difference?" replied the rustic, "sexful and successful are one and the same thing."

Contributed by J.P. Singh Kaka, New Delhi

*K*ARVA *Chauth* could best be described as India's Husbands' Day. Most Hindu and Sikh women, whether or not happy in their *Suhaag* (matrimony) fast and pray for their husband's good health and long life. I know of a lady who spends most of her time in an *ashram* return to her philandrous husband on *Karva Chauth,* touch his feet and perform his puja. When I asked her why instead of fasting and praying for him she did not live with him, she replied bluntly, "I can't stand his company for more than an hour."

A SIKH couple was always quarrelling with each other, however, when it came to *Karva Chauth,* the Sardarni Sahiba decked herself in all her finery to go to the Gurudwara."Why are you dressed up like a bride and where are you going?" asked her husband angrily.

The Sardarni Sahiba snapped back: *"Tera hee siapa karan challi haan*—I am going to perform your funeral ceremony."

Contributed by P.N. Sachdev, New Delhi

A MAN went to a *dhaba* run by a Sardarji and ordered a full *tandoori* chicken. When the bird was placed before him, he asked. "How is it that this chicken is short of one leg?"

The *dhaba* owner replied, *"Aap nay chicken khanna hai, ya iskay saath dance karna hai?* (You want to eat it or dance with it?)"

Contributed by J.P. Singh Kaka, New Delhi

A DELEGATION of Sikhs called on the former Prime Minister, Rajiv Gandhi. "The police always makes us Sikhs stand in the background at your public meetings. All other communities are given VIP treatment and allowed to stand in front," they complained.

The Prime Minister reassured them. "Don't worry, as soon as we have a war on our hands, I'll see that you Sikhs are put in the front of all other communities."

*T*RYING to show off familiarity with foreign languages can land you in difficulties. There is the well-known case of a British Minister on a visit to Moscow who, in order to please his hosts, mugged up a short speech in Russian. On his way to the banquet he realised he did not know the Russian for 'ladies and gentlemen.' He stopped his car near a public lavatory and took down the Russian equivalent. His speech did not get the kind of applause he expected. Afterwards he asked one of his colleagues what had gone wrong. The colleague replied, "your speech was excellent. But why did you have to start with 'Male and female urinals'?"

*T*HIS anecdotes relates to Maulana Shaukat Ali's close association with Mahatma Gandhi during the days of the Khilafat agitation and their subsequent parting of ways.

Gandhiji often addressed meetings from Khilafat platforms. Audience which were largely composed of Muslims wanted to know why a Hindu Bania had taken up the cause of the Caliphate which was entirely a Muslim affair. Being a tall and stout man, Maulana Shaukat Ali would have a dig at Gandhiji: "He is a small man: I have him in my pocket."

Later Shaukat Ali quit the Congress and joined the Muslim League. "Where is that Mahatma Gandhi who had promised to get us Muslims our rights?" Maulana Shaukat Ali would ask at every public meeting. The Mahatma replied to the question at one of his prayer meetings: "The Maulana wants to know where I am. He used to say he had me in his pocket. Let him look inside and he will find me."

Contributed by Jalal Zakaria

A RUSSIAN technical expert was being shown round one of our steel plants. "How is it," he asked, "that despite all the new machinery we give you, your output keeps declining?"

"We have union troubles. And strikes," replied his Indian escort. "Last year we had to shut down for a month."

"We have no strikes in our plants," said the Russian proudly. "We do not allow workers to put down tools."

"How nice!" commented the Indian. "But then you do not have to contend with Communists as we have to."

*A*GHA Shahid Ali, a Delhi-born Kashmiri, is almost unknown as a poet in his homeland. He deserves to be taken seriously. I give two samples of his composition. This one is entitled, 'Today, talk is cheap. Call somebody...'

I called Information Desk, Heaven, and asked, "When is Doomsday?" I was put on hold.

Through the hallelujahs of seraphs, I heard the idle gossip of angels, their wings beating rumours of revolts in Heaven. Then I heard flames, wings burning, then only hallelujahs.

I prayed, "Angel of love,
Please pick up the phone."
But it was the Angel of Death. I said, "Tell me,
tell me, When is Doomsday?"
He answered, "God is busy.
He never answers the living.
He has no answers for the dead. Don't ever call again, correct."

In another poem 'Language Games', he has witty-macabre lines like:

You challenged me to Charades I agreed. This would be my syllable-cure.
Tableau One: I licked a saucer of milk.
You cried : CAT!
Tableau Two, I was stubborn as a mule.
You cried : ASS.
Tableau Three : I gave you my smile, like a prize.
You cried : TROPHY.
You cried : CAT-ASS-TROPHY?

MANY foreign visitors prefer to travel by train because they feel they get to know the country and the people better than those who go by bus or airplanes. But since they have a tight time-schedule, their sight-seeing has often to be drastically cut because of the chronic unpunctuality of our trains. An American tourist who had made train bookings to all the towns and cities he meant to visit, found himself in a quandry. When the conductor came to check his ticket, he exploded, "Why the hell do you print a railway time-table if your trains never run on time?"

"Sir," replied the railway official calmly, "the time-table will tell you how late your train is running."

Contributed by Dr. S.K. Saxena, Jaipur

THE November '88 issue of *Span* has an interesting episode on Nehru's life recounted by J.K. Galbraith who was the U.S. ambassador in Delhi. A much married Hollywood filmstar called on the Prime Minister.

"Well, Miss Dickinson," Nehru said, "when you are featured in a movie that takes two months or more to film, I suppose you become deeply involved in the role you are playing. Does that have a lasting effect on your character or personality?"

Nehru was delighted with Angie's reply: "In my last three movies," she said, "I have played the part of a woman of questionable morality. I hope that has not permanently affected me."

Contributed by N.K. Niketan

*A*N amorous lass by the name of Pamella
Claimed to have loved many a fella
From businessmen to MP's
Alleged spies to VIPs
Causing Maggie's Government to turn a pale yella.

Contributed by Rajeshwari Singh, New Delhi

*A*N Air Force officer was killed in an air crash. He went straight to heaven. It so transpired that a week later his orderly was killed in a train accident and was also admitted to heaven.

When the Air Force officer saw the orderly, he shouted, "Ganda Singh, why are you so late?" "Sahibji," replied the orderly, "You are entitled to air travel so you came by air. I am a class IV servant only entitled to rail travel; so I had to come by train."

Contributed by J.P. Singh Kaka, New Delhi

A PROUD father was very upset with his son's report card. The boy had been given a zero for English spelling. He confronted the teacher and demanded an explanation. She calmly asked the boy to write the word "coffee" on the blackboard. The boy wrote out, *kauphy*. "You can see for yourself how bad his spelling is", said the teacher very triumphantly.

The boy's father refused to give in. "He has at least got the number of letters right; six in each case. You could have given him some credit for that."

Contributed by Lt. Col. S.R. Garkhel, Bareilly

*T*HERE was a man with lots of money in his bank. He was stricken with cancer and the doctors gave him just six months on earth. He had no relations and was eager to take his life's savings with him to enable him to live well in the next world. He consulted his friends and asked them how he could fulfil his wish. They told him it could not be done. But a lawyer said it was very simple. If the dying man transferred all his assets to the lawyer, he (the lawyer) would make out a cheque for the full amount and send it to him as soon as he died. This is exactly what he did. As soon as the man died, the lawyer made out a cheque in the name of the deceased's payee account. It was cremated with the corpse.

Contributed by S.K. Bhalla, New Delhi

A POOR man sat outside a temple begging for alms from worshippers: "In the name of *Bhagwan* give this hungry man some paise to fill his belly. *Bhagwan* will bless you." But people went to pray in the House of God, gave the poor beggar so little that he had never enough to buy *daal-roti*. In sheer disgust he quit the temple and sat outside a *theka* where people came for their evening *paaooa* of *desi*. "A few paise in the name of *Bhagwan*," he whined, as people came out in high spirits. Instead of paise many dropped rupees notes in his begging bowl. The beggar gave thanks to God in the following words: "Hey *Bhagwan*: truly inscrutable are Thy ways! You give one address but live in another place."

OF all the modes of travel we have in our country, riding a bus in Calcutta must be about the most hazardous. Whenever I see them crammed beyond human endurance with dozens of people hanging by the windows, I marvel at the Bengalis' tolerance of inhuman conditions. I've never seen them brawling or even using strong language. Dr. Arunava Chattopadhyay ascribes it to the Bengalis' sense of humour and quotes some of the graffito he has seen in Calcutta buses. To wit: Beware of Ladies pickpockets; girls and children above five years must have full tickets; To shit 30+2.

THERE was a computer scientist from London
Who had with binary digits lots of fun
When asked his age
Replied the sage
'I'm 100 001.'

There was a young prodigy from Sevagram
Who was muttering PQR....in his pram
Said a guest, "He's precocious"
Replied his father, "Yes!"
These days he's studying electrocardiogram."

Contributed by Dr. Aggarwal, New Delhi

AFTER almost half a century in journalism, I am still unable to gauge in advance how readers will respond to a particular article. Who besides crackpots like me would be interested in road signs? I was surprised by the number of letters from distant parts of the country on the subject. This might lead one to conclude that as a nation we are very conscious of road safety. That is far from being true. From the limited number of cars we have our record of accidents is about the worst in the world. Over 4,000 are killed and thousands more seriously injured on our roads every year. The worst record is of the city with the widest roads, Delhi!

From amongst the contributions I have received, these are some of the more witty ones:

Road sign : "Be cautious; road in dangerous condition. Survivors will be suitably punished."

"Jaldi karti kaam kharab/Hosh mein aao laat sahab—haste spoils things you will see/come to your senses Mr. V.I.P."

Contributed by Shashank Shekhar, Meerut

Warning (against drunken driving):
'There are three menaces to safe driving: hic, hike, hug.'

Contributed by Kailash Bahl, Delhi

A signboard before a sharp curve: 'Expect the unexpected.'

Contributed by C.K. Raveendran

Rear of a bus: 'Overtakers, beware of undertakers.'

Contributed by P.R. Krishnan

Road signs: 'If brakes not fit, you'll land in shit'.
'Driving faster can cause disaster.'
Warning sign against drunken driving: 'Drink and drive, you won't survive.'

Contributed by Rajeshwari Singh

Notice (outside a liquor vend): '*Theka sharab desi:* Price per bottle Rs. 25, concessional rate for bus/truck-drivers.'

Contributed by Neelam Yadav, Ambala

Boards on a highways: 'Mountains are a pleasure; only if you drive with leisure.'
'Drive with care, make accidents rare.'
'Your hurry may cause my family worry.'
'Always alert, accidents avert'
'Keep your nerves on a sharp curve.'
'Drive on horsepower, not on rumpower.'
'Darling I want you but not so fast.'

Contributed by Bhavna Mathur, New Delhi

Car sticker: 'Make love not war; see the driver in the car.'

Contributed by Jamshed Siddique, Aligarh

Board on the road:
'If married, divorce speed.'

Contributed by Yudhvir Singh Goyal, Faridabad

Road Sign: 'It is better to be 15 minutes late in this world than be 15 minutes early in the next. Speed: 15 miles per hour.'

Contributed by Dr. Ashok Pant, Nainital

Note of caution :
'Be slower on earth than quicker to eternity.'
'If you want to donate blood, do not do it on the road. Donate it in the blood bank.'

Contributed by S.K. Bandopadyaya, Calcutta

Road signs:
'Fast won't last.'
Board near a girls' hostel:
'You are not watching the road.'

Contributed by Reeten Ganguly, Agartala

Board on a highway: 'Be soft on the curves.'

Contributed by Ravi Soni, New Delhi

Road Sign: 'Love thy neighbour but not while driving.'

Contributed by Kaval Kapoor, New Delhi

Road signs: 'Don't dream, otherwise, you will scream.' 'If looking for survival, don't believe in fast arrival.'

Contributed by D.K. Jain, Delhi

Pinned to the board of a bus: 'If you sleep, your family will weep.'

Car bumper: 'A cat has nine lives, but not the one which drives.'

Contributed by T.R. Rishi, Jaipur

MORE than other agricultural communities, the Jats have been singled out as targets in anecdotes and proverbs for lack of sophistication. *Jat maluk vasalaan da ujaara*—though a Jat becomes refined, it is onions that he will devour, or *Jat maluk trua rumaal*—even a refined Jat will use a mattress as his handkerchief. He has no head for figures and is the living embodiment of *sola doonee aath*—sixteen times two make eight. But he has a hearty laugh: *Jat da haasa, tey ghareeb da bhanney paasaa*—Jat's laugh breaks the ribs of poor mortals. He is notorious for his reluctance to pay his debts: "When he ploughs his land he will take a loan, when he watches his crops he closes his eyes, when he harvests his yield, he forgets his moneylenders."

Among non-Jat Punjabis, it was regarded wise to keep Jats in shackles: *Jat tey phat baddha changa*—a wound and a Jat are best kept bound. And, of course, he is so tough that you must not believe he is dead till after the 13th day of his obsequies: *'Jat maria taab jaaneeyan jo tehrveen ho jai.*

A COMPLIMENT I have to often suffer from my fans is the way they gush and mispronounce the word malice. Many of them pronounce it as mal ice: *"aap ka malaees parh kar bahut anand aayaa."*

Two sisters Minakshi and Jyoti Jha of Patna have written of a similar mispronunciation of the word nature. An inspector wrote the word on the blackboard and asked his students to read it aloud. All of them pronounced it as *natoor.* He was appalled. He write the word future on the blackboard and pronounced *"Tum sab ka footoor kharaab hai*—you have no future."

*H*ERE are some examples of anagrams of names of celebrities:

1. Former Prime Minister Rajiv Gandhi=I hear he is driving—in a jet

2. Vishwanath Pratap Singh=Ah VP's wrath—pigs in Thana.

3. Devi Lal=Live lad

4. NT Rama Rao=Rat on a Ram

5. Surjit Singh Barnala=Lush Ragis inn—Jat Bar

6. Menaka Gandhi=Aha—King and me?

7. Margaret Thatcher=Charm at the garter

8. Benazir Bhutto=A broth is ze tub

9. Jyoti Basu=Joy is Buta!!!

10. Amitabh Bachchan=Baba can hatch him

11. Bal Thackeray=Bharat Lackey

12. Khushwant Singh=Hug'n kiss'n what!

Contributed by Pushi Chowdhry, Chandigarh

110

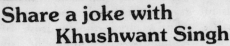

Share a joke with Khushwant Singh

If you have a joke, a humorous anecdote or a funny incident, which is original and you would like to share it with Khushwant Singh and his million admirers, send it to us today. If selected, it would be printed in the next edition of Khushwant Singh's Joke Book.

... and a million others

Remember

- Each joke or anecdote must be neatly typed or written on a separate sheet of paper in about 125-150 words.

- Do not type or write on both sides of the sheet. Write on one side only.

- Send your jokes to :

    Khushwant Singh's Joke Book
    c/o **Orient Paperbacks**
    Madarsa Road, Kashmere Gate
    DELHI - 110 006

- Each contribution received would be acknowledged.

- Each selected contribution would be acknowledged and included in the next edition of **Khushwant Singh's Joke Book** along with the name of the contributor.

A POLITICIAN delivered a powerful oration to his party members. His audience was overwhelmed and rushed to felicitate him when he had finished. Some asked for his autograph, others garlanded or touched his feet. A journalist who wanted the address of his newly constructed bungalow asked him, "Sir, can I have your telephone number?"

"For that you have to ring me up," replied the politician.

Contributed by A.R. Kapur, Lucknow

A LEAD article devoted to science in *The Hindustan Times* having the printer's devil with only one letter (L from 'black') missing makes a whale of a difference:

"Back holes are really neither 'black' nor 'holes' in the general connotation of these terms. In fact, they are quite contrary to what the term 'holes' seems to imply. Because of their popularity in public parlance, they have come to be accepted as scientific terms too."

Contributed by Parvez Akhtar, Patna

I CAME across a clipping from *The Tribune* inserted by a lady asking for a loan. For obvious reasons I have to withhold the name of the lady. The ad runs as follows:

"Wanted Rs. 5000 only for one year for shifting business to a centrally located place. Can also negotiate sleeping partnership."

Contributed by Subhash Kaushik, Ludhiana

ALTHOUGH separated by half a century in years, Meena Sinha doing her Ph. D. in Hindi and Sanskrit from Delhi University and I share a common passion: collecting slogans written behind vehicles. She specialises in three-wheelers which she uses every day. I have never sat in one and they go past at such a speed that I miss most of what is written on them. She, on the other hand, prefers to hire those which carry wit on their rear, and when travelling by bus, will get off it just to catch a three-wheeler on which something inscribed has caught her eye. She has quite a formidable collection. I quote a few which I had not noticed. Some are variations of the perennial theme *buree nazar say dekhney vaaley, tera munh kaala*— you with the evil eye, may your face be blackened!

How about this:

Buree nazar vaalaa too mera saalaa—

You with the evil eye, I have married your sister.

Married is an understatement for other designs on the sister of evil eyed. Or:

Buree nazar vaaley, nasbandee kara ley—

You of the evil eye, have yourself sterilized.

What he really means is that you should be castrated. Then there is this one giving tit for tat:

*Buree nazar vaaley, teyrey bachchey jeayen
Badey ho kay teyra khoon peeyen.*

You of the evil eye, may your children live long.
And grow up to suck your blood.

Some are couched in riddles. For example: "*Ek baar muskara*—2, meaning "*ek baar muskara do* — smile at me for once." Or name of the vehicle's joint-owners: "Maneesh, *100 Desh,* Prince, *V-kee kee gaddi*—this belongs to Maneesh, Sudesh, Prince & Vikki."

A MAN took a clipping of a newspaper and read it out to his friend: "You know what this says? It says that a man divorced his wife because she was in the habit of going through his pockets."

"What are you going to do with the clipping?"

"I'll put it in my pocket."

Contributed by Bano, New Delhi

A UNIT of the army was posted on the border. Came Janam Ashtami and the *jawans* set up a temple with the statue of Shri Krishna for worship. They invited their commanding officer to inaugurate the prayer session. The commanding officer inspected the temple and asked, "In every Krishna temple there is always Radha by his side. Why have you left her out?"

"Sir," replied a quick-witted *jawan*, "because this is a non-family station."

Contributed by Dr. Khosla, Jalandhar

A HARYANVI peasant who was charged with theft went to engage a lawyer. "How much money have you got to pay my fee?" asked the lawyer.

"*Gareeb aadmee hoon, Sahib*—Sir, I am a poor man. All I have is a tractor," replied the peasant.

"If you have a tractor, you can't be very poor. You can raise money on it and pay me," said the lawyer. "What have you been accused of stealing?"

"Sir, the tractor"

Contributed by Shashank Shekhar, Meerut

*T*HERE was a Punjabi couple who were connoisseurs of good food. They were invited to a dinner party by a friend. The man knew some English: his wife none at all. On their way back home after dinner the wife made disparaging remarks about the quality of the food in Punjabi: "*Palak-paneer* was *thud*(third) class. Even the *Gajar ka halva* was like *kicchad* (mud)."

Her husband agreed with her opinion. "Nothing was good except the catering."

"*Accha*". Replied the wife, "*Oh tay main chakkhia hee nahin*...I didn't as much as taste the catering."

Contributed by Anita Sharma, Bombay

A PANDITJI who had presided over all religious functions in the village decided to quit in search of greener pastures. He summoned the village *panchayat* and explained his reasons for quitting: "Firstly, you do not love me because you give nothing for my upkeep. Secondly, you do not love each other and I have had no marriage ceremonies to perform. And finally, even God does not love you because He has not summoned any of you for a long time since I did not have a single funeral to conduct.

Contributed by Shivtar Singh Dalla, Ludhiana

A MINISTER was the chief guest at the finals of a football tournament. After giving away the prizes, he was requested to say a few words. He said, "It pains me to learn that this year only two teams could make it to the finals. When we have hundreds of football clubs in the country, we should endeavour to see that many more teams reach the finals next year."

Contributed by J.P. Singh Kaka, New Delhi

*O*NCE upon a time there was a preacher who wanted to collect money for the church. He was told that horse-racing was the quickest way of getting it. So he went to a horse auction but finding the bids too high, bought himself an ass. He entered it in the local races. To everyone's surprise the donkey came in the third position. The next morning, the papers had headlines on their sports pages reading: "Preacher's ass show."

Encouraged by the donkey's performance, the preacher entered it for the next race. It romped in first. The next morning's papers carried the headlines: "Preacher's ass in front."

The bishop was outraged and ordered the preacher to get rid of the animal. The preacher dutifully gave it to a nun. The papers heard of it and reported the event in the headlines: "Nun has the best ass in town."

This time the bishop was furious and ordered the nun to dispose of the animal. She sold it to a farmer for ten dollars. The next day, the papers reported: "Nun peddles ass for ten bucks."

Contributed by P.M. Ayappa

*T*HE lady minister of Rajasthan in a speech delivered in March 1988 accused the Opposition of not cooperating with the administration even on programmes like control of population. Replying to her speech, a member, Sawant Singh, said: "The lady minister believes that if the Opposition extended its cooperation, population could be reduced. But our experience has been to the contrary. Whenever opposite parties cooperate with each other, population increases."

Contributed by B.S. Rayal, Delhi

*B*ANTA SINGH migrated to England but could not find a job. He also failed to learn English. His friend Santa Singh suggested he sell potatoes and learn three sentences by rote. "When they'll ask you how much? You reply: "One pound per kilogram". Then they'll ask you if they are good, you reply, "Maybe, may not be." Some will buy them. To those who do not, you say, "You not take, some other will take."

The formula worked and Banta's business flourished. One day an American lady tourist came by and asked Banta the way to Picadilly Circus. "One pound per kg," replied Banta.

"Are you nuts?" asked the American lady angrily.

"Maybe, may not be."

"I should be taking you to a loony bin," said the American hussy in a temper.

"Madamji," replied Banta, "If you no take, some other will take."

Contributed by J.P. Singh Kaka, New Delhi

118

*T*HIS incident relates to pre-partition days. Mr. Singh had to catch a train from Amritsar to Lahore. He got to the station in the nick of time. The guard was waving his green flag and blowing his whistle. He rushed to a compartment where a man was standing in the doorway and asked to be let in. "No", replied the man, "Can't you see it is ladies' compartment?"

"Forgive my mistake," replied Mr. Singh, "I took you to be a man."

Contributed by Pritam Singh, Jalandhar

*T*HE Seoul Olympics in which the USSR was on top of the medal tally and India at the bottom, opens up new avenues of Indo-USSR collaboration. We should list certain disciplines in which the two countries should participate in setting up joint ventures so that we can win a medal or two with their help. Why spend crores of rupees on sports and come back empty-handed?

Contributed by S.K. Rampal, New Delhi

A YOUNG English lady visiting India picked up as much Hindustani as she could during her stay. She did, however, mix up some of the vocabulary including the words *chaprasi* and *chapatti*. Giving an enthusiastic account of a meal in a gourmet restaurant, she wrote to her mother, "Dear Mom, last night I had a lot of *chaprasis*. They were delicious. But if you have too many of them, they are apt to lie on your chest all night."

Contributed by Harjeet Kaur, New Delhi

A KINDLY gentleman wanting to befriend a family which had moved into his neighbourhood spoke to the youngest son: "*Beta*, how many brothers and sisters are you?"

"Sir, we are nine brothers and three sisters," replied the youngster.

"And *beta*, tell me what does your papa do?"

"*Ji, voh yahee kartey hain* (sir, this is all that he does)."

Contributed by J.P. Singh Kaka, New Delhi

A PUNJABI gentleman living in Delhi had to go to Saharanpur in U.P. He rang up railway enquiries and got train timings and fares for Delhi-Saharanpur. Then he rang up the Inter State Bus Terminus and got all the bus timings and fares for the same journey. Buses were more frequent and the bus fare was cheaper than rail ticket. However, after much thought, he opted to go by train. "Why?" asked his friends.

He replied without batting an eye-lid, "I made further enquiries and found out that the railways pay higher compensation for death caused in an accident than State Roadways."

SOUNDS of a terrible quarrel were coming out of a house. A crowd of curious passers-by collected. Suddenly the door opened and a small boy ran out. *"Beta,* what is the trouble?" asked one of the crowd. "Are your parents fighting?"

"Jee haan, they are always fighting."

"Who is your father?" asked the man.

"That's what they are always fighting about," replied the boy.

Contributed by Shashank Shekhar, Meerut

ONCE I took a party of South Indian friends to see the Golden Temple after *darshan* I took them to the temple kitchen, *Guru Ka Langar.* As soon as the *thalis* were laid out before the eaters, they began, as is customary, to chant *Satnaam-Waheguru.* Then the *sewadars* came shouting *veerjee, roti* (brother, chapatti), *bhainjee, daal* (sister, some *daal*). The party having enjoyed the food, one of the South Indians asked, *"Roti* and *daal* were served, why not *veerji* and *bhainjee?"*

Contributed by D.S. Malik, New Delhi

THE contents of a signboard on the door of a lawyer's chambers which reads: "Where there is a will there is a way; where there is a way there is law; where there is law there is a rule; where there is a rule there is a loophole; where there is a loophole there is a lawyer, and here I am Mr. so & ... advocate."

Contributed by Sudhee, New Delhi

*A*N irate Haryanvi father whose son had ploughed in his arithmetic examination took issue with the teacher.

"Your son is a *budhoo* (dull), replied the teacher. "I put him a simple question: If you have two bananas and I give you another two, how many bananas will it make?" He replied, "three.".

"Just for one miserable *kela* you fail my son!" roared the angry sire. "Here is a *chavani* (25 paise) for a banana. Now pass my son."

Contributed by J.P. Singh Kaka, New Delhi.

R.E. Canteenwala gets malicious pleasure in translating foreign names to get a laugh. A Chinese friend named, Who Flung Dung, was addressed as 'Flying lump of shit.' Most unkind!

Names in one language can often be very uncomplimentary in another. Canteenwala should know that the common Indian surname, Das, means turd in Swedish. The commonest Scandinavian surname, Lund, and the name of the German Parliament, Bund, refer to the fore and aft of the human anatomy in Hindustani. Then there was the South Korean ambassador, who later became Foreign Minister, whose name was Bum Suk Lee. What about Canteenwala? How would it sound as *bawarchikhaneyka?* His own community, the Bawajis, provide the funniest sounding names in India.

A MAN rushed into a police station and asked to be arrested for assaulting his wife with a *chimta* (fire-tongs).

"Did you kill her?" demanded the officer on duty.

"No," replied the man, "*Isee liye to yahan aaya hoon*—that's why I have come here. Take me into protective custody."

Contributed by Shashank Shekhar, Meerut

*P*LACEBO It means something which cures every ailment. Or is prescribed by a doctor when he runs out of ideas. Harish Monga of Ferozepur writes of a rich hypochondriac who was constantly pestering his doctor for medical check-ups and demanding medicines for his imaginary illnesses. Ultimately, the doctor devised a code prescription: ADT. Another doctor happened to be present in the clinic. He asked what the prescription meant.

"Any damn thing," came the reply.

*B*ASED on writings behind many trucks is the following amusing anecdote. A Sardarji truck-driver emigrated to England. His knowledge of English was limited to the few words printed on the back of his vehicle—"O.K., tata, and see you later *(phir milangey).*

He was invited to a meal by fellow truck-driver who had emigrated earlier. As he was about to leave, his host bade him farewell with the similar words, "O.K., tata, *phir milangey.*"

The new arrival promptly responded, "horn please."

123

*F*OUR workers were discussing how smart their dogs were. The first was an IBM employee who said his dog could do maths and calculations. His dog was named "T Square", and he told him to go to the blackboard and draw a square, circle, and triangle, which he did with no trouble.

The Ford employee's dog was named "Side Rule". He was told to go fetch a dozen cookies, bring them back and divide them in four piles of three each, which he did. The C & P employee said that was pretty good, but he told his dog, "Measure" to go buy a quart of milk and divide it into equal parts into three glasses. He did it perfectly.

The three of them agreed their dogs were pretty smart and they all waited to see what the Federal Government employee's dog, who's name was "Coffee Break" could do. At the snap of his owner's finger, "Coffee Break" strolled over at the cookies, drank the milk, screwed the other three dogs, claimed he injured his back, filed a workman's compensation form and went home on sick leave.

Contributed by Amir C. Tuteja, Washington

A CURD vendor (*dahiwala*) was travelling in a bus with his pot of curd. He was sitting on a seat which was meant only for ladies. On a subsequent stop some ladies got in & asked him to vacate the seat for them. When the *dahiwala* asked "why?" then one of the ladies replied in Hindi, *"Hum mahilayen hain, isliye."* The *dahiwala* didn't understand and replied, *"To kya hua, hum bhe dahilayen hain."*

Contributed by K.V.S. Partha Sarathi, Calcutta

124

ONCE a drunkard spent all his money in the bar with his friend. When he was left penniless, he staggered home with his friend to get more money from his wife. They staggered into the bedroom to switched on the light. They saw the wife making love to a stranger. The drunkard politely asked his wife for some money. His wife shouted at him "take it from my purse. But for Pete's sake turn off the lights." The man took money to pay for two pegs and turned off the lights. When they (the friend and the drunkard) came out of the house, the friend asked, "What about the guy in the bed?"

Prompt came the reply, "He can buy his own drink."

Contributed by Deepika Seth, New Delhi

A HARYANVI peasant went to a lawyer to fight his case. The lawyer readily undertook to do it but was curious to know why the peasant had come to him. "Did people tell you to come to me because I was a good lawyer" he asked.

"Naa bhai Sahib," replied the peasant honestly, "I consulted many lawyers before coming to you. They all said, *"Koi bewakoof hee thaaraa case lad sakai sai*—only a fool would take up your case."

Contributed by Shashank Shekhar, Meerut

*I*N the fifties, there was a rickshaw-puller, an ex-serviceman, who lived near my house in Himayathnagar. Once while I was going to Nampally, in his rickshaw, I got talking to him. I said, *"Lala Miyan,* you say you lost your wife two years ago and that you have four children to look after. Why don't you go in for a second marriage?"

Turning his face towards me, he said, *"Saab, izzat aur aabroo se zindagi guzar rahi hai. Doosri shaadi ki kya zururat hai."* (Sir, I am pulling on in life with *izzat* (dignity) and *aabroo* (honour). Where is the need for a second marriage?)

I thought he didn't want to have a stepmother for his children, and so I quickly changed the topic. But later, I was surprised to learn from his friends that he was having affairs with two beautiful dames named, Izzat Begum and Aabroo Begum.

Contributed by Judson K. Cornelius, Hyderabad

*B*ANTA Singh was living in a DDA ground floor flat with his 12 children. A family planning motivator called on him and asked him somewhat acidly, "Banta Singhji, how is it that you have so many children?"

"Sab ooper vaaley dee maya hai—It's all the gift of the One above—" he replied, pointing to the roof.

The family planning man promptly went to the first floor, got hold of Santa Singh who occupied the premises and had his *nasbandi* done.

Contributed by J.P. Singh Kaka, New Delhi

A HIGH-level delegation led by the chief secretary of a certain north Indian state was on a visit to Kenya. The delegation, among the other high-ranking officers, had a DIG of police—an IPS officer known for the *darbardari*.

The Kenyan government put at their disposal a small plane for their safari. During the flight, the engine failed and the plane, while making an emergency landing, struck a tree. The members of the delegation were, however, unharmed.

The police officer hugged the chief secretary and started crying like a child. The chief secretary consoled the police officer but he would have none of it.

"God has saved us. Come on, you are a police officer, you should not cry," said the chief secretary.

The police officers replied. "Sir, it would not matter if I had died, but what would happen to our state if we had lost you."

Contributed by J.L. Manwati, Bombay

A FAVOURITE joke is about the respective efficiencies of the secret service agencies. "The K.G.B. is tops," boasted a Russian. "It has been able to get all the designs of the latest American weapons produced in the last 10 years."

"Our C.I.A. has done better," retorted the American. "It has stolen from the Kremlin results of the Soviet elections for the next 10 years to come."

A COUPLE of weeks ago I received an anonymous letter from Islamabad containing an unsigned poem entitled, "A User's Guide to Indian Causology." I found it extremely witty and biting in its satire. I reproduce it in full for Indian readers."

When the monsoon fails and the sun drums down
On the parched Gangetic plain
And the tanks dry up and dust storms blow
Where once were fields of grain.
When hunger stalks each village hut
And famine grips the land,
It isn't Mother Nature's fault—
It is the Foreign Hand!
For this is India, you see,
Not Germany or France,
And nothing here is blamed on God
Much less on quirky chance.
Here evil has a fingered form
Both alien and planned.
It is that darkly subtle limb—
It is the Foreign Hand!
When Hindu lads hack Sikhs to death
In peaceful Delhi town.
When Rajiv's corns are acting up
Or the Bombay bourse goes down,
When the pesky little Nepalese
Insist on things like borders.
When once-tame Tamil Tigers balk
And taking South Block orders.
The reasons for this mischief
I think you'll understand
It's those meddling foreign digits—
It is the Foreign Hand!
So when you're in a Delhi lift

Beside a buxom dame
And you give in to the natural urge
To pinch her husky frame,
Confront her adamantine glare
With a visage mildly bland,
And say: "It wasn't me, my dear—
"It was the Foreign Hand!"

*S*AID a nagging wife to her husband: "Do you realise how old our Banti is? Seventeen, going on to eighteen. Have you even bothered to look for a suitable match for her?"

"I do, I do," protested the husband "But every boy I interview on her behalf turns out to be a *bewakoof*—idiot."

"If my parents had been as particular about me as you are about our daughter, I would have remained unmarried all my life," retorted the wife.

Contributed by Raheem un-Nissa Bakshi, Belgaum

*B*OFORS here, and Bofors there,
Bofors in the air everywhere,
Political buffaloes when they pass wind,
Lo, the sound *"bhoo fas!"* so *"Jai Hind."*

Contributed by R.E.C. Canteenwala, Lucknow

130

A LARGE number of anti-Russian jokes are manufactured by the jews who continue to be discriminated against in Communist Russia. Thousands have sought permission to emigrate to the States. Rabinovich applied for an exit visa. "You have everything you need in Soviet Russia," said the visa officer. "Why do you want to leave?"

"I have two good reasons for wanting to leave," replied Rabinovich. "The first is that my neighbour comes home drunk every evening and swears that as soon as the Communists are overthrown, he and his nationalist Russian friends will hang all the jews."

"Surely, you must know Rabinovich, that Communism will never be overthrown," said the visa officer.

"That," replied Rabinovich, "is my second reason, for wanting to go"

*S*INCE Gorbachov took over, Vodka, the favourite beverage of the Russians, has become a scarce commodity. There was a mile-long queue outside a liquor store. "I can't take this any more," said Ivanov. "I am going to get my pistol and shoot Gorbachov."

Two hours later Ivanov was back to rejoing the queue. "What happened?" asked the others still in the line.

"I decided to get back here," replied Ivanov. "The queue outside Gorbachov's apartments waiting to kill him is longer than this one."

*T*HE son of a Haryanvi businessman had agreed to join the family business, and on his very first day at the factory, his father took him on to the roof and said, "Now, *beta* (son), I am about to give you your first lesson in business. Stand on the extreme edge of the *'chhat'* (roof).

"On the edge! *Pitaji*," asked the perplexed junior.

"Yes, on the very edge."

"Very well, *Pitaji* (father)," and the obedient *beta* did as he was told.

"Now, when I say "Jump," said the Haryanvi, "I want you to jump below."

"But, *Pitaji!* It's a twenty feet drop !"

"*Beta*, no *'lekin-vekin'* (excuses)," said the 'true-businessman' Haryanvi. "Dont you trust me? If you really want to learn the twists and turns of business, do what I say"—And the Haryanvi yelled "Jump!"

And the junior jumped, only to crash painfully to the ground twenty feet below. The Haryanvi ran down the stairs to where the poor soul was lying-bruised, battered and winded. Chirped the Haryanvi, *"Beta, aaj tanne business mein apna pehla sabak seekh liya sai.* (Son, you have just learnt your first lesson in business)—NEVER TRUST ANYBODY.

Contributed by Shashank Shekhar, Meerut Cantt.

A LITTLE urchin selling newspapers had many bundles on his head and in his arms. A kindly passerby asked him : *"Beta,* don't you get tired of carrying so much load?"

"Not at all, sir," replied the boy cheerfully. "I don't have to read them; I only sell them."

From Bano—contributed by Farzana Furqan, Lucknow

NEXT to picking up jokes about politicians, I like collecting anecdotes about men of religion showing them in a poor light. Neither are difficult to find as both professions attract the most loathsome dregs of humanity and have much in common: all politicians are preachers and all preachers dabble in politics. Anyone who puts them down deserves an accolade.

My favourite put downer of holy humbugs is from Louis XIV's sister-in-law, the Duchess of Orleans. Her hero was a 17-year-old boy in a Jesuit school who was often thrashed by the Catholic brothers who taught him. To teach them a lesson, the boy went to an artist and persuaded him to paint two pictures on his buttocks: Saint Francis Xavier on the left and Saint Ignatius on the right.

Back at school he misbehaved in his usual rowdy manner and was summoned by the headmaster (a Catholic Father) to receive corporal punishment—caning on his bare buttocks in front of the entire school. The boy fell on his knees and cried loudly, "O Saint Francis, O Saint Ignatius, have pity on me and perform a miracle and save me from punishment because I am innocent."

As his trousers were pulled down for the beating, the two Saints revealed themselves on the seats of punishment. According to the Duchess of Orleans, the Jesuit teachers fell on their knees and saluted the boy's buttocks with kisses. A real life miracle if ever there was one.

SOME people think the longer it is the better. Others believe that since it is only a label for identification, the shorter the more convenient. Thus we have the erstwhile Governor of Jammu & Kashmir describing himself in a one-word name, Jagmohan. And the new Member of Parliament from Darjeeling likewise is simply Inderjeet. People from the south like to include their father's name, their caste, as well as the name of their village in their names. Bengalis, though not so long-winded about their names, do not think that you should ever drop your caste surname. Thus you have Banerji, Chatterji, Mukherji, Ganguli etc.—or at times hyphenated two-in-one like Das-Gupta, Sen-Gupta or Roy-Chowdhury. Natarajan Anand of Howrah writes to say that whenever he introduces himself to Bengalis as Anand, their immediate reaction is *"eto choto naam—how can you have such a short name?"* To oblige them he added Iyer to his Natarajan Anand. Even this made his Bengali friends uneasy, that there was something missing. So he added the names of his grandfather, father as well as his horoscope to it: "I am Khizambor Ramainen Natarajan Srinivasan Iyer," he replied when asked his name.

"Eto bodo naam—such a long name?" they asked.

PAKISTAN *se doosra Test khatam honey ko hai— 'Faisla baad' mein."*

Contributed by Tagore Sharma, Chandigarh

134

*A*N office circular makes an interesting reading. "Mr Virender Ganda is the Secretary of the Company. It has been noticed that many people mispronounce his surname "Ganda" by pronouncing first part 'Gan' as rhyming with the word 'Ram' or the English word 'ran'. But the correct pronunciation is as rhyming with the English word 'gun'. The way it is mispronounced, the word has unseemly meaning in the Punjabi language. It is, therefore, requested that everybody may take note of the correct pronunciation as the officer feels rather embarrassed by the mispronunciations."

Contributed by O.P. Malhotra, New Delhi

*T*HE five rules of socialism:
Don't think.
If you do think, don't speak.
If you think and speak, don't write.
If you think, speak and write, don't sign.
If you think, speak, write and sign, don't be surprised.

From 'No Laughing Matters' by Seigel

A SCHOOL teacher asked his students to use the Hindi expression *Karey Karai peh paani pher diya* in a sentence to explain what it meant. A bright lad replied "after urinating he pulled the chain and flushed it down."

Contributed by Suneeta Bhudhiraja, Noida

135

I SAW an invitation card of a wedding that took place in Madras last November. South Indians have charming abbreviations of titles. The bridegroom's full entitlement *chiranjivi* is reduced to *chi;* the bride suffers a worse fate being reduced from a *Sowbhagyavati* to a porcine *Sow*. The card though from Madras is of a marriage between Bengalis settled there. The bride, Mittu is a Bishwas. The bridegroom Subhas has an uncommon and malodorous family name being the son of Shrimati and Shri Mahadev Shit of Bankura, West Bengal. From enquiries it is discovered, the Shits originated from Bihar and migrated to Bankura. They were scavengers who carried night-soil of generations of indigo planters named West. In appreciation of their services the Shits were granted three villages in Bankura district. The Shits are allowed to wear the sacred thread and are perfectly respectable *bhadralok*. They should find solace in the fact that upper caste Brahmins like the Dixits or Dickshits get similar reaction in England where their caste-name means bird-droppings.

Contributed by Dev Ashish, Madras

T HE factory owner in Punjab asked his manager to get a gun for the *chowkidaar*.

"We shall have to first procure a licence for that sir," the manager pleaded.

"Nonsense!" shouted the old man—"AK–47 requires no licence in Punjab."

Contributed by Kaminder Suryavanshi, New Delhi

*T*HE son of a Haryanvi was being taught the twists and turns of business by his father. The Haryanvi told his son not to take any decisions for himself but merely watch him closely and observe his methods of handling business.

One day, a customer arrived at the Haryanvi's shop. The junior Haryanvi asked his father, "*Pitaji* (Father), there is a customer outside who wants to know if our guaranteed non-shrink sanforized shirts will shrink."

The Haryanvi asked, "Does the shirt fit him?" The junior replied in the negative, "No; it's quite large."

"Then,"told him the Haryanvi,"*shrink hongi sai* (It will shrink)."

Contributed by Shashank Shekhar

*O*NCE two Congress party leaders, Poppat Lal and Tota Ram, happened to meet each other. Poppat Lal was boasting of his immense love for the work of upliftment of women's status in the society like this: "The other day I was passing through a *mohalla* when I saw a man beating his wife mercilessly. I was red with anger. I went to that brute and said indignantly, "You bloody rascal! What the hell you are upto? Only a coward can resort to beating a woman like this. If you are a real *surma* (courageous fellow), try your hands on a *mard* like me."

"*Achha* (okay)!What happened later?" asked Tota Ram out of sheer curiosity.

"*Uske baad kya hua, mujhe kuchh yaad sa nahin,*" (I don't remember as to what actually happened afterwards) chirped Poppat Lal.

Contributed by Shashank Shekhar

A HARYANVI having drained his bottle of *desi* to the last drop was standing by the side of a road. When a pedestrian came along he asked him: *"Bhai sahib*, where is the opposite side of this road?"

The pedestrian pointed to the other side and replied, "Over there". The inebriated Haryanvi lost his cool, *"mhara paagal bannaavey sai* (you want to make an ass of me?) When I asked the same question to a passerby on the other side, he sent me here."

Contributed by Shashank Shekhar, Meerut

T HERE was a truck-driver who took guidance from messages written behind public vehicles: He never cast an envious eye (*buree nazar*) on anything desirable. Then he came upon advice which he took to heart:

Beewee rakkho goree goree
Do kay baad choree choree

(Let your wife be the fairest of the fair. After two keep them in secret).

He divorced his not-too-*goree* wife and married another who was as *goree-chitti* as the full moon. Then his eye fell on the truck owner's daughter, also milk-complexioned. So he eloped with her. Whenever asked why he had done so, he replied:

Beewee rakkho goree goree
Do kay baad choree choree

Contributed by Bishen Swaroop Aggarwal, Ropar

CHAUDHARY Devi Lal was taking a stroll one evening when he met a man much bigger than himself coming from the other side. Chaudhary Sahib could not resist asking. *"Arrey! too kaun sai—who are you?"*

"I'm God," replied the man.

"Kaam kya karai sai—what do you do?"

I give people birth and I make them die when I want to."

Chaudhary Sahib could not accept anyone being more powerful than himself. So he threw God a challenge. "Let me see if you can make me die."

The same evening the Chaudhary Sahib was relaxing on his charpoy when a beautiful lady dressed in white visible only to the Chaudhary Sahib came in and sat down by his pillow. The Chaudhary Sahib felt there was something very odd about the lady and quickly took the pillow to the other side of the charpoy. The lady quickly went and sat by the pillow. They went on doing this for quite some time when the Chaudhary Sahib's sons noticed him changing sides on the charpoy every few seconds and decided that there was something going wrong with him. So they brought a long rope and tied their father down to his charpoy. Suddenly God appeared on the scene and asked Chaudhary Sahib what he had to say. *"Teyrey say to kabhi na dabta—you could never have overcome me"* replied Chaudhary Sahib, *"merey beyton nay hee mujhey dabaa daala—my sons have been my undoing."*

Contributed by Vineet Khanna, Chandigarh

139

No sooner was General Zia buried than a whole lot of anti-Zia jokes which were whispered around began to be told openly. "How did they recognize General Zia's body from the debris of the air-crash? It was the only one firmly clutching the chair it was seated on."

The other one is more macabre in its black humour. Since all victims of the crash were mutilated beyond recognition, the workers putting bodies in coffins did the best they could, giving each a head, torso, arms and legs, without bothering what belonged to whom. The bodies were solemnly interred in different graves, General Zia's in a yet to be built mausoleum in Islamabad.

The General was summoned by God and reprimanded for the wrongs he had done to the people. "You will receive a hundred lashes on your buttocks," was the divine sentence.

The General was duly tied to a post, his bottom exposed and the jailer began to apply the whip. With each stroke, the General roared with laughter. The Almighty was very surprised at his behaviour and asked, "Why are you laughing while being beaten?"

"Because the buttocks receiving the lash belong to the American ambassador."

A BJP leader was asked to explain the meaning of present-day democracy.

He replied, "Government off the people, Government far from the people and Government to buy the people is called DEMOCRACY."

Contributed by Jasbir Singh Bindra, Ludhiana

SOME birds have very suggestive names. There is, for instance, one named yellow bellied sapsucker: a charming little feathered fellow common in Canada and the United States; its human incarnation more common in India than elsewhere. Then there is another with an even more suggestive name, double-breasted tit: common in human species all over the world. Knowing my predilection towards soft porn, Jemini Rumba of Shillong has suggested that dirty old men like me, who indulge in watching both feathered and human (female variety) birds, instead of being called ornithologists, should be called chick-watchers or hornithologists. Very apt!

THIS back-handed tribute to the filmstar Rekha won the first prize in the St. Stephen's College winter fest in 1981.

There was a lass called Rekha.
Who thought all males were eager to take her.
If only she knew
That there were so few
The truth, I am sure, would shake her.

This one was composed on the slimming fad amongst the opulent:

There was a man from Delhi
Who had a massive belly.
He started to slim
Until they couldn't see him.
And now he's lost in the melee.

Contributed by Anup Verma

A POTATO-DEALER was very proud of his son, Ramu. One day he claimed before his neighbour that his son, Ramu was very clever and his brain was very clear. The potato-dealer exclaimed, "Do you know the other day his Headmaster on the way told me your son, Ramu has got very clear head; whatever lecture I deliver in the class, it straight away reaches to one of his ears and passes through his head and comes out from the other ear, nothing is retained in his head."

Contributed by Dr. Gaurisankar Mukherjee, Kanpur

WHEN Kamraj Nadar was Congress President, he used to come to Delhi for attending meetings, conferences etc. At that time, he used to stay with Pandit Nehru. During the course of breakfast, lunch, dinner etc, Kamraj Nadar used to impress upon Pandit Nehru the comfort of wearing *lungis*. "It is very convenient to go to bathroom and walking in the garden, lying down in bed etc." He promised to send a dozen *lungis* to Pandit Nehru from Madras.

Pandit Nehru got angry and replied: "Mr. Nadar, *lungis* are for you South Indians. If I wore a *lungi*, how will I do *shirshasana?*"

Contributed by P.V. Nayak, New Delhi

AN interview was conducted by the assistant editor to recruit new staff for the paper. The question-and-answer session went somewhat as follows:

Who has the best batting average among the current Indian cricketers?

Azharuddin.

The first Indian expedition to the Antarctica was led by:

Dr. Z.A. Qasim.

Who designed the missile *Agni?*

Dr. Abdul Kalam.

Who is the national champion in tennis?

Zeeshan Ali.

Who is the Asian snooker champion?

Yasin Reza Merchant.

Name the India-born author who won the Booker Prize?

Salman Rushdie.

Now name the best in:

Hockey—Mohammad Shahid.

Poetry—Ali Sardar Jafri.

Acting—Naseeruddin Shah and Shabana Azmi.

Economy—Abid Hussain.

History—Irfan Habib.

Dialogue writing—Dr. Rahi Masoom Raza.

Journalism—M.J. Akbar.

"All Muslims? What are Hindus doing in Hindustan?" asked the interviewer.

Contributed by Shahid A. Chaudhary, Meerut

143

*T*HERE is something about Urdu poetry that makes people burst out into *wah! wah! Muqarrar, Irshad,* etc. even before the poet has finished reciting the first line. Most of the time they don't even comprehend the meaning of what is being said. I found an amusing illustration of this in the humour column (*Tabassum*-smile) in an old copy of Sadia Dehlavi's magazine *Bano*.

A well-known poet was invited to read his latest composition. He came upto the microphone, opened his notebook and began:

"Two shirts and two *patloons.*"

Wah! wah! came the applause.

"Three vests and a sari," continued the poet.

"*Irshad! Bahut khoob*", came the applause.

The poet stopped, turned over the notebook and exploded, "What the hell are you applauding me for? Instead of my poetry notebook, I've brought the dhobi's account book."

*I*T is said of the poet Ghalib that once when he was in dire straits; with no money to buy provisions for the home, his wife advised him to go to the mosque and pray to Allah for help. Ghalib did as he was told. At the entrance to the mosque, he ran into one of his drinking companions who persuaded him to come along to the tavern. He returned home very late. When his wife asked him why he was so late, he replied, "Allah answered my prayer at the door step of the mosque. So I went to the *maikhana* to give him thanks."

Contributed by B.S. Kalra, Delhi

"My teacher must be very religious," said the little girl. "Every time I answer one of her questions she says, "My God! My God!"

Contributed by Angshuman Chakraborty, Darjeeling

Two young Bengalis were taken to a Haryana police station for having beaten up a shopkeeper. "What are your names?" growled the Haryanvi *thanedar*.

"Chatterjee," replied one. "Bannerjee", replied the other. Thanedar Sahib lost his cool. "You are goondas and yet attach *jee* to your names!" he thundered. "Put down their names as Chatter and Banner," he ordered his clerk.

Contributed by Minakshi Jha, Patna

The following lines on Salman Rushdie makes an interesting reading :
The Satanic Verses
Have drawn many curses
And death threats for Rushdie galore
His alleged blasphemy
Has brought him infamy
And caused an international furore
So Rushdie is hiding
His time he is abiding
But it seems he's been marked for life
And only a miracle
Or a change-of-heart clerical
Can prevent widowhood for his wife.

Contributed by Rajeshwari Singh, New Delhi

Sawai Man Singh Medical College and Hospital, Jaipur, celebrated its golden jubilee of establishment with much fanfare. A life science exhibition was on during the entire celebration period of one month. Entry ticket to this section was Re 1. One of my friends asked if there was anything free of cost. I suggested him to go to room number 31 and find out for himself. He went there and found a big board reading: "Post-mortem is done here free of cost. Please do not pay any bribe to anyone for the post-mortem."

Contributed by Dr. S.K. Saxena, Jaipur

One day a smart Alec pulled up his car in the middle of the road and began a loud dialogue with his girlfriend, standing on the balcony of the fourth floor of a building. An elderly gentleman stopped his car a few yards from the youngman's, walked up to him and asked very politely: "Could you tell me how to get to Dr. Peter Dias Road?"

"This is it," replied the youngster cheerfully.

"Tell me, does Dr. Peter Dias happen to be your father?"

The message got home.

Contributed by J.L. Manwati, Bombay

An American Red Indian went into a bar in Chicago and ordered himself a drink. A white American sitting next to him on the stool asked him, "And how do you like our city?"

"Fine," replied the Red Indian. "And how do you like our country?"

A POPULAR anecdote told is about a *Mujahir* (emigrant from India pejoratively described as *tiliyar*—starling because of it chittering too much) arriving in paradise. He demanded immediate attention of the Almighty and clamoured for justice: "All-powerful Allah, I was shabbily treated in Pakistan. First it was the Punjabis who bullied us poor *mujahirs* who voluntarily left Bharat to settle in Pakistan; then it was the Sindhis who made us feel unwanted; and now it is the Pathan *Mujahideen* who are doing us out of business. And once again it is the Punjabis who are after our blood. They are the worst of the lot. They keep all the jobs for themselves and treat us as unwanted foreigners. When we protest they shoot us down. I came to you as *Shaheed* (martyr). I deserve a place in paradise and want you to punish these wicked, godless Punjabis."

Allah pondered over the matter and then ordered his angel secretary in *theth* Punjabi: "*O is bandey dev failaan taan liayeen*—get me this fellow's files."

A WOMAN went to lodge an FIR at the police station. "My husband went to the market to buy potatoes two days ago. He has been missing since then."

"Why bother?" replied the SHO. "You can cook another vegetable."

Contributed by Yog Babu, Aligarh

*T*HIS anecdote is about political parties employing *goondas* to rig polls. The *goonda* fraternity had its own undercover identifications to establish its political credentials. The police got a wind of it. So when it arrested four hoodlums they were ordered to stand in line.

"Raise your *dhoti*," ordered the police officer.

The first man had a red *langoti*. "Lock him up, he is communist," ordered the official.

The second wore a green *langoti*. "Lock him up, he is a Majlis Ittehad-e-Musalmeen."

The third had a saffron underwear. "Lock him up, he is BJP."

The fourth who didn't have any underwear, explained his nudity as "an independent without political affiliations." He was set free.

Moral: do not wear *langotis* till elections are over.

Contributed by K.R. Unnikrishnan, Trivandrum

A GOVERNMENT official was arrested for accepting a bribe from a contractor. A friend who went to visit him in the lock-up asked, "How are you going to get out of this mess?"

The official replied calmly, "I got into trouble for accepting a bribe; I'll get out of it by giving it."

A MANAGER of a branch bank found he had no space left to store old records. He wrote to his regional manager for permission to destroy old records. The regional manager wrote back: I do not mind your destroying old records but please make sure you keep photo-copies of all destroyed papers."

Contributed by Vir Inder Singh, Gurgaon

A MAN went to see a doctor, *"Daktar Sahib,"* he complained, "I am suffering from a strange disease. When I walk, my one foot is always ahead of the other."

The doctor gave him two pills, "Take one after you have gone to sleep; the other before you get up."

Contributed by Razia Sultana, Warangal

A VERY old widow had an only son. Everytime he brought a present for her, she would say "Son keep it for visitors— *aaiya gayey layee.*"

Then she arranged a marriage for him. It was a disaster as the son did not take to his bride. His mother tried to persuade him: "Take her out with you somewhere where she can be alone with you," she pleaded.

"No Ma," replied the son, "let her stay at home—*aaye gayey layee.*"

Contributed by K.L. Dutta, Dehra Dun

I DON'T know whether there is such a thing as a Day of Reckoning after death. For men of religion, I quote an anecdote. Someone asked a friend, notorious for drinking, if his brother who was a priest raised any objections to his heavy consumption of liquor. He replied, "We have a very good relationship. He prays for me, I drink to his health."

Contributed by Reten Ganguli, Tezpur

A GAMBLER'S three-year-old son learnt to count upto thirteen. It went as follows: *Ek, do, teen, chaar, paanch, chhey, saat, aath, nau, das, ghulam, begam, badshah.*

Contributed by J.P. Singh Kaka

TWO men who had recently emigrated to a foreign country were boasting about their skill in befooling others. "None can surpass me in this art," said Lehna Singh.

"How is that?" asked Banta Singh.

"I have befooled the government," replied Lehna Singh. "I've come to this country on a return ticket and I am not going back," he added, with a twinkle in the eye.

Contributed by P.S. Dutta, Chandigarh

*H*ERE is a contrived anecdote about Dr. Bidhan Chandra Roy who was an eminent physician before he became Chief Minister of Bengal. I cannot vouch for its ...thenticity.

It is said that once Dr. Roy was travelling by bus when ...ang of robbers boarded it and began to loot the ...sengers. When they came to Dr. Roy, he asked, "Will ...rob your own elder brother?"

...hey *pranaamed* him and got off the bus. When the ...engers looked suspiciously at Dr. Roy, he disclosed his ...tity, "I am Dr. Bidhan Chandra. I am a Congress ...er and have donations given by party members with ...I did not lie to the robbers. Listen to this sloka:

Vaidyaraja Namastubhya,
Tvam Yamraj Sahodarah
Yam to harti pranani, tvam
pranani dhanani cha.
O doctor, Salutations to you,
You are elder brother of the
God of death,
Yama only takes our lives,
You take both our lives and
our money."

Contributed by Vijay Bharadwaj, New Delhi

A CARD buyer went to buy Christmas and New Year's cards. He also wanted a birthday greetings card to send to a friend. Having bought his quota of the Yuletide variety he failed to locate a birthday card and asked the dealer to find him one. "I am sorry, sir," replied the dealer, "this is not the birthday season."

Contributed by Reeten Ganguly, Tezpur

Dear Reader,

Welcome to the world of **Orient Paperbacks**—India's larg
selling paperbacks in English. We hope you have enjo
reading this book and would want to know more about O
Paperbacks.

There are more than 400 **Orient Paperbacks** on a variet
subjects to entertain and inform you. The list of aut'
published in **Orient Paperbacks** includes, amongst othe
distinguished and well-known names as Dr. S. Radhakrishn
R.K. Narayan, Raja Rao, Manohar Malgonkar, Khushw
Singh, Anita Desai, Kamala Das, Dr. O.P. Jaggi, Nor
Vincent Peale, Sasthi Brata and Dr. Promila Kapur. **Ori
Paperbacks** truly represent the best of Indian writing in Engl
today.

We would be happy to keep you continuously informed o.
new titles and programmes of **Orient Paperbacks** through
monthly newsletter, **Orient Literary Review.** Send in your na
and full address to us today. We will start sending you **Orie
Literary Review** completely free of cost.

Available at all bookshops or by VPP

ORIENT PAPERBACKS
Madarsa Road, Kashmere Gate
Delhi-110 006